# PROBLEMS IN THE PRINCIPLES OF ACCOUNTING

BY

WILLIAM MORSE COLE, A.M.
ASSOCIATE PROFESSOR OF ACCOUNTING
IN HARVARD UNIVERSITY

CAMBRIDGE
HARVARD UNIVERSITY PRESS
1915

## ACKNOWLEDGMENT

The author wishes to express his indebtedness to Professor Donald English, of Cornell University, to Dr. Joseph S. Davis, of Harvard University, and to Miss Lolita E. Healey, of Radcliffe College, for painstaking assistance in reading the proof of this volume, for suggestions as to the best form of stating the problems, and for confirmation of the correctness of the answers or cues given.

# CONTENTS

## APPENDICES

# PROBLEMS IN THE PRINCIPLES OF ACCOUNTING

## INTRODUCTION

THE problems in the following pages have been prepared to afford students ready means of testing with actual figures their knowledge of accounting principles.

The aim is in only slight degree to afford the sort of mechanical practice that results in facility, though some degree of facility must spring from any practice; the prime aim is to afford material on which the student may cultivate the power and the habit of seeing straight, of seeing deeply, and of seeing whole. All serious accounting work requires the accountant to do these three things: first, to see the surface meaning of things; second, below the surface facts to see the underlying facts; third, to see the relations of all the fundamental facts to one another. Except for the bookkeeping problems — in which, moreover, the aim is as far as feasible the same as in the accounting problems, — the exercises following are intended to demand of the student careful observation (to show him what the figures mean), or the application of some analytical power (to tell him what lies below the surface), or sense of relationship (to indicate to him how present figures are tied up with other figures). Many of these problems require the exercise of all three of these faculties at once.

Either of two methods is feasible for the choice of material for exercises, — actual figures yielded in specific business enterprises, or imaginary figures devised to call into play certain lines of thought on the part of the student. The former gives the student a certain degree of familiarity with actual figures, and, if a sufficient number of cases is taken, with normal figures; but a very large number of cases is usually needed to cover the specially noteworthy conditions, for few sets of actual figures chance to combine many notable facts. Then so much of the student's thought is occupied with the repetition of mechanical processes that he loses alertness for the recognition of differences in principle. When imaginary sets of figures are taken, on the other hand, each may combine several notable features and so give the student the maximum opportunity for the use of his intelligence with the minimum expenditure of time in examining and recording conditions that are already an old story to him. To a great extent, therefore, resort is made here to imaginary sets of figures, and no care is taken to avoid the unusual circumstance; for always enough of any set of figures is normal to give the student familiarity with the appearance of normality, and to give him practice both in identifying the unusual thing in the midst of normal things and in seeing its bearings analytically and synthetically. To say of any set of figures, then, that it represents a very unusual situation is not to say that it is not worthy of study, but may be to say that it is most useful because one can see in it, in full effect, the virtue or the evil of some important accounting theory or practice. Just as one in common talk can often best make clear one's point by an illustration intrinsically absurd, so one can often show most clearly an accounting principle by figures intrinsically improbable.

This would not be true if the aim in teaching accounting were to teach specific facts about business, or specific methods of procedure for certain kinds of circumstance. No one can ever understand accounting by learning how specifically to do specific things. The conditions and the happenings and the modifying circumstances of modern business are so multitudinous that no lifetime is long enough for one to learn by rule what should be done in every kind of case. Accounting is nothing but sublimated common sense applied to interpreting the facts of business. The requisite for accounting is simply intellectual vision with the ability to express the truth intelligibly. Such vision and such power of expression are best cultivated by practice in handling not merely the usual and stable (certainly not merely because they are usual and stable), but rather the peculiar and the unique, for these force the student to work out for himself methods and processes that may be capable of numerous applications in circumstances which, though on their faces they are wholly unlike, are in essence of the same sort.

These problems have been designed for use with the author's "Accounts: Their Construction and Interpretation," published by Houghton Mifflin Company, of Boston. They therefore follow the same order of treatment of subjects as that book, which, though it appears to give much discussion of specific lines of business, does so only in order that it may illustrate the fundamental principles of accounting in the fields where they may be most profitably studied. At the head of each group of problems in the following pages is given, for the convenience of those using that book, the designation of a passage in which are discussed the principles involved in the problem. All but a few of these problems are possible of solution by persons familiar with accounting principles but unfamiliar with that text: the few exceptions will be sufficiently obvious; they follow some suggestions for accounting methods not at present in general practice. In the main, all work is cumulative: the references given for each set of problems presuppose that all previous references are familiar to the student. One should not expect to pick a problem at random and merely by consulting the reference cited in connection with that problem learn how to solve it. To large degree the work is a unified whole, and often the treatment of the peculiarities of one distinct type of business is made to hinge on the previously discussed peculiarities of another type in many respects wholly unlike it. For students who desire to get a comprehensive grasp of fundamental principles, this is the most economical procedure.

# DEBIT AND CREDIT

[Chapter II [1]]

[1] The references are to the author's *Accounts: Their Construction and Interpretation: Revised and Enlarged Edition.*

## 1

Determine for the following transactions whether the account named in parenthesis is to be debited or to be credited. For the purpose of testing the correctness of your work, list all the debits in one column and all the credits in another, and then compare the totals with the cue given at the end of the problem.

(*a*) Receiving cash for a debt due to the business (Cash), $2,500.
(*b*) Selling merchandise (Merchandise), $2,400.
(*c*) Receiving a promissory note in payment of a debt due to the business (Bills Receivable), $2,450.
(*d*) Paying John Smith $2,333 owed to him (John Smith).
(*e*) Paying $2,267 in cash for wages (Cash).
(*f*) Buying merchandise for $2,250 (Merchandise).
(*g*) Receiving cash for interest due to the business (Interest), $148.
(*h*) Paying $297 for commission (Commission).
(*i*) Buying an office safe for $318 (Office Furniture).
(*j*) Paying $46 for postage (Postage).
(*k*) Selling merchandise for $326 (Merchandise).
(*l*) Receiving of John Brown a loan of $1,583 (John Brown).
(*m*) Paying rent (Cash), $158.
(*n*) Borrowing $1,265 on a promissory note of the business (Bills Payable).
(*o*) Paying $140 for expenses (Cash).
(*p*) Paying debts of the business (Cash), $5,104.
(*q*) Receiving $4,457 due to the business (Cash).
(*r*) Receiving from John Robinson $4,950 owed by him to the business (John Robinson).
(*s*) Paying expenses (Expense), $2,425.
(*t*) Borrowing on a note (Cash), $1,265.

[The total of each column, debit and credit, should be $18,341.]

## 2

For the following transactions determine — regarding both the debit and the credit — whether the entry should be made to a property account, a force account, or a personal account. Then provide for six columns as follows: Property, Dr.; Property, Cr.; Force, Dr.; Force, Cr.; Personal, Dr.; Personal, Cr. For each transaction below enter the amount in one debit column and one credit column — corresponding to the proper debit and the proper credit to be made for the two accounts concerned in the transaction. Then compare your totals with the cue given.

(*a*) Buying merchandise for cash, $3,215.

(*b*) Receiving a promissory note for a debt due to the business by a customer, $1,367.

(*c*) Paying wages in cash, $873.

(*d*) Buying merchandise on credit, $2,792.

(*e*) Selling for somebody else goods on which you are allowed a commission of $326 (now to be entered on the books as due to you).

(*f*) Setting off against an amount due to you by one of your customers interest on money borrowed by you from that customer, $139.

(*g*) Incurring a bill for advertising, $75.

(*h*) Buying real estate for cash, $8,500.

(*i*) Receiving cash for rent on a building owned, $300.

(*j*) Retaining, as a loan from employees, wages already earned by employees but not previously entered as earned or paid, $680.

(*k*) Paying for merchandise, which was previously bought and entered to the account for merchandise and to that for the firm of whom it was bought, $1,634.

[The property debits should be $16,174; property credits, $14,222; force debits, $1,767; force credits, $626; personal debits, $1,960; personal credits, $5,053.]

## 3

The following pairs of debits and credits were made as a result of certain transactions. Analyze each, assuming that the name used for each account sufficiently indicates the nature of that account, and show the final net result of all transactions, on (*a*) the amount of property in the business, (*b*) the loss or gain of the business, (*c*) the claims against it or in its favor.

| Debit | Amount | Credit |
|---|---|---|
| Merchandise | $1,312 | John Smith |
| Wages | 259 | Cash |
| John Brown | 518 | Commission |
| Wages | 90 | John White |
| Cash | 834 | John Robinson |
| Interest | 108 | Cash |
| Rent | 200 | Interest |
| John Smith | 1,000 | Cash |
| Commission | 85 | Cash |
| John Jones | 75 | Interest |
| Cash | 327 | John Jones |

[The increase in property is $1,021, the net gain is $51, and the increase in liabilities (or decrease in favorable claims) is $970.]

## DEBIT AND CREDIT IN THE FUNDAMENTAL BOOKS

[Chapters III and IV]

### 4

Make entries in simple journal form, for the following transactions, assuming that the items before January 11 are on page 15 of the journal and that later items are on page 16. Then post these entries, giving a different page number to each ledger account by beginning with page 25 for the first debit, taking page 26 for the first credit, page 27 for the second debit, etc.; but, of course, carry a second posting for the same account to the same page number.

Jan. 1. The proprietor invested cash in the business, $5,000.

Jan. 4. Paid in cash one month's store rent, $100.

Jan. 6. Bought for cash, 500 barrels of flour at $5.00 per barrel.

Jan. 8. Sold George Spring & Company, on account, 55 barrels of flour at $6.00 per barrel.

Jan. 10. Bought of William Winter, on account, 100 bushels of corn at 35¢ a bushel.

Jan. 15. Sold to James Summers, on account, 10 barrels of flour at $5.80 per barrel.

Jan. 18. Paid wages of clerk, $12.

Jan. 22. Received rent for desk-room in office, $25.

Jan. 26. Paid $40 for a harness for delivery equipment.

Jan. 27. Received from George Spring & Company their note for $330, for their bill of Jan. 8.

Jan. 29. Borrowed $2,000 on a note of the business for $2,000.

[The following should be the totals of the ledger accounts:

| Page | Dr. | Cr. |
|---|---|---|
| 25 ............... | $7,025 | $2,652 |
| 26 ............... | | 5,000 |
| 27[1] ............... | 100 | 25 |

[1] The student may find that his page 27 includes what is here given separately on 32, and that the $25 here included in page 27 is carried by him separately. If so, his page numbers will be obviously affected.

| Page | Dr. | Cr. |
|---|---|---|
| 28 | $2,535 | $388 |
| 29 | 330 | 330 |
| 30 | | 35 |
| 31 | 58 | |
| 32 | 12 | |
| 33 | 40 | |
| 34 | 330 | |
| 35 | | 2,000] |

## 5

Show by journal entries what should be debited and what credited on the books of Arthur and on the books of Burt for the following transactions, when 6 % is assumed as a fair rate of interest:

(*a*) Arthur lends Burt in cash the value of a promissory note for $1,000, payable in four months, and bearing interest.

(*b*) Burt pays the above note at maturity.

(*c*) Arthur again lends Burt cash on a note, but this note, though for the same amount and with the same term, does not bear interest.

(*d*) Burt pays the above note at maturity.

(*e*) Arthur sells Burt merchandise for $1,000, with payment due in two months; Burt gives in part payment his note for $500, due in two months.

(*f*) When the balance of Burt's bill is due, he obtains from Charles a $500 promissory note, payable two months in the future but dated two months in the past, and bearing interest; this note he delivers to Arthur; then Burt pays his own note previously given Arthur; any balance due one or the other party in the settlement is paid in cash.

(*g*) Charles pays the above note at maturity.

(*h*) Burt buys $500 worth of merchandise of David on account.

(*i*) David draws a $500 draft on Burt (which Burt accepts) and gives it to Arthur in payment for goods — both the goods and the draft requiring payment in one month.

(*j*) At the maturity of the above draft, Arthur buys some land of Burt for $500, and Burt tells Arthur in payment to send Burt's own acceptance to Charles; when this is done, Charles presents it for payment, and Burt pays it, with interest of $15 on Charles's loan to him.

Post these items to Arthur's ledger and to Burt's ledger.

[Arthur's ledger will show a net credit to Interest of $45, and Burt's will show a net debit of $50. Arthur's Bills Receivable will have total debits and credits of $3,500 each, and Burt's Bills Receivable will be square at $500, and his Bills Payable at $3,000. Arthur's cash will have increased $1,045, and his real estate $500; and his merchandise will be credited $1,500. Burt's cash will show a decline of $1,050, and his real estate and merchandise the reverse of Arthur's.]

## DEBITS AND CREDITS TESTED BY THE TRIAL BALANCE

[Chapter V to page 39]

### 6

Post the following items to the ledger, find the final balances of all ledger accounts, and take a trial balance of those balances.

November 1

| | | |
|---|---|---|
| Cash .................... | $7,500.00 | |
| To Proprietor ......... | | $7,500.00 |
| 2 | | |
| Mdse. .................... | 3,000.00 | |
| To Cash ............. | | 3,000.00 |
| Customers ................ | 57.60 | |
| To Mdse. ............ | | 57.60 |
| Proprietor ................ | 50.00 | |
| To Cash ............. | | 50.00 |
| 3 | | |
| Cash .................... | 100.00 | |
| To Mdse. ............ | | 100.00 |
| 4 | | |
| Mdse. .................... | 137.00 | |
| To Creditors .......... | | 137.00 |
| 5 | | |
| Creditors ................. | 77.50 | |
| To Cash ............. | | 77.50 |
| Mdse. .................... | 65.30 | |
| To Creditors .......... | | 65.30 |

6

| | | |
|---|---|---|
| Customers ................ | 475.25 | |
| To Mdse. ............ | | 475.25 |
| Cash .................... | 29.70 | |
| To Customers ........ | | 29.70 |
| Mdse. .................... | 500.00 | |
| To Creditors .......... | | 500.00 |

8

| | | |
|---|---|---|
| Customers ................ | 320.00 | |
| To Mdse. ............ | | 320.00 |
| Proprietor ................ | 28.00 | |
| To Cash ............. | | 28.00 |
| Customers ................ | 17.50 | |
| To Mdse. ............ | | 17.50 |

[The total of the trial balance should be $8,046.80.]

## 7

Enter the following transactions in the journal, post them, and take a trial balance.

You as proprietor invest $10,000 in cash, and $5,000 in notes bearing interest (with interest already accrued to the amount of $28).

Buy goods of T, on account, $3,000.

Pay $600 for stationery.

Sell B goods, on account, $3,000.

Pay T, $1,000.

Receive of B his note for $2,000.

Buy goods of S, $7,000; give note for $5,000, and pay $2,000 in cash.

Pay personal tailor's bill out of the cash drawer, $100.

Buy goods of R, on account, $10,000.

The notes invested by you are paid, with interest, the total amounting to $5,050.

Pay note given S, with interest, $50.

B pays cash, $1,000.

Give to T the note of B which you hold.

Lend A $4,975 on his note for $5,000 due in 30 days.

How do your affairs now stand, according to the books, with T, B, S, and R? Is this as it should be?

[The total of the trial balance of ledger *balances* should be $24,928, or $100 more if a separate account is kept for proprietor's drawings.]

## 8

Journalize the following transactions, post, and take a trial balance.

Invest in business as follows: cash, $10,000, and notes of F, $6,000, not bearing interest, worth $5,900 when discount is allowed for.

Buy merchandise of B on trust, $18,000.

Pay B $6,000 cash, and give him your own note, bearing interest, for $12,000.

Sell to C merchandise, $1,000 payable in one month, and receive from C his note for $1,000, payable in two months, and cash, $5.00.

$2,000 is collected on notes of F.

Sell merchandise to C for $13,000, and get in payment notes for $12,800, bearing interest, with interest accrued to the amount of $200.

Take up note given to B, now amounting with interest to $12,100, and give in payment some of the notes received from C, $11,800, with interest accrued to the amount of $300.

Pay wages by cash realized from discounting at a bank your own note for $500, payable in 30 days.

[The total of the trial balance of ledger balances should be $16,502.50.]

## 9

Write the following transactions in journal form, post them, and take a trial balance.

Nov. 21. Partner A invests $10,000 cash.

Nov. 21. Partner B invests bonds worth $9,500, with interest accrued to the amount of $20, and office furniture and equipment worth $480.

Nov. 22. We give a second-hand office typewriter, supposed to be worth $50, in payment for advertising in the program of an exposition.

Nov. 23. We sell goods for another firm, and earn a commission of $25; but as Partner A owes that firm interest amounting to $25, the two firms agree to set one debt off against the other.

Nov. 24. We buy goods of Green & Bros., $2,000.

Nov. 25. We sell goods to Delay & Co. for $350, and they pay $200 on account.

Nov. 26. We sell goods to Gray & Son for $2,000.

Nov. 28. We exchange the bonds which B invested, $9,500 at par, with interest accrued at $28, and merchandise at $772, and cash $1,200, for a building worth $11,500.

Nov. 29. For Brown & White we sell property amounting to $6,000, and collect the cash from the purchaser; we are entitled to a commission of $450; but we pay bills for advertising, preparatory to the sale, amounting to $45 (not chargeable to Brown & White), and for transfer and record fees amounting to $25 (chargeable to them).

Nov. 30. Green & Bros. draw on us a draft payable to Gray & Son for $2,000. By agreement with Gray & Son, we cancel their debt to us in exchange for the draft.

If the inventory of merchandise is $28, and no business has been done but that indicated here, what is the profit or loss for merchandise, for interest, for commission ?

[The total of the trial balance of ledger balances is $27,105; the combined profit of merchandise, interest, and commission is $1,633: but if the second advertising item ($45) is charged to Commission, the total of both the trial balance and the profit accounts will be less than the amount given. The reason for charging the special advertising to general advertising in this case is that it is presumed to have an effect of general publicity.]

## DETERMINING PROFIT AND LOSS FROM THE BOOKS

[Chapter V, pages 40–45]

### 10

Balances are found on ledger accounts as follows:

| | |
|---|---|
| Proprietor | $50,000 |
| Bills Receivable | 18,000 |
| Bills Payable | 8,000 |
| Real Estate | 35,000 |
| Cash | 3,000 |
| Wages | 8,000 |
| Expense | 2,000 |
| Merchandise | 8,000 |

The following inventories are given:

| | |
|---|---|
| Real Estate | $33,000 |
| Expense (supplies) | 500 |
| Merchandise | 10,000 |

The following item is found accrued but not due:

| | |
|---|---|
| Wages liability | $750 |

Construct the six-column statement, and show the proof.

[The total of the liability column is $58,750, and of the loss column is $12,250. (Those who use a different form of statement, omitting the proprietor's credit balance from the liabilities, will have a correspondingly reduced figure for the liability column.)]

### 11

Show and prove the six-column statement for the figures on the following page.

*Ledger totals*

| | Dr. | Cr. |
|---|---|---|
| Cash | $175,000 | $170,000 |
| Merchandise | 138,000 | 128,000 |
| Customers [1] | 148,000 | 126,000 |
| Creditors [1] | 137,000 | 141,000 |
| Real Estate | 35,000 | 2,000 |
| Fixtures | 8,000 | 1,000 |
| Depreciation | 4,000 | |
| Expense | 23,000 | |
| Interest | 1,500 | 500 |
| Commission | 1,000 | 2,000 |
| Proprietor | | 100,000 |
| | $670,500 | $670,500 |

*Inventories*

| | |
|---|---|
| Merchandise | $57,000 |
| Supplies | 200 |

*Accrued items*

| | |
|---|---|
| Interest earned | $200 |
| Commission liability | 100 |

*Prepaid items*

| | |
|---|---|
| Insurance (charged to Expense) | $100 |

[Total of liability column, $104,100; of gain column, $47,900. (See the notation in the cue to Problem 10.)]

[1] Totals of all such accounts.

## 12

Fill out the following incomplete six-column statement, using no figures not given or *implied*, and prove it.

| | Dr. | Cr. | Resources | Liabilities | Loss | Gain |
|---|---|---|---|---|---|---|
| Cash . . . . . . | .... | .... | $20,000 | | | |
| Office Furniture . | $3,000 | .... | .... | .... | $500 | |
| Expense . . . . . | 13,000 | .... | .... | .... | 13,000 | |
| Interest . . . . . | 500 | .... | .... | .... | .... | $50 |
| Bills Receivable . | .... | .... | 5,000 | | | |
| Bills Payable . . | .... | .... | .... | $2,000 | | |
| Customers . . . . | 3,000 | | | | | |
| Creditors . . . . | .... | $1,000 | | | | |
| Merchandise . . . | 20,000 | .... | .... | .... | .... | 21,000 |
| Capital Stock . . . | | | | | | |

[The net gain is $7,550.]

## CLOSING THE BOOKS

[Chapter V, pages 45–56]

### 13

Construct a ledger to show the balances given in Problem 10. Then make the additional ledger entries for closing the books at the end of the year, as indicated in the problem, close the ledger, and show the balance sheet.

[The total of the balance sheet will be $64,500.]

### 14

Construct a ledger to show the balances given in Problem 11. Then make the additional entries for closing the books, as indicated in the problem, close the ledger, and show the balance sheet.

[The total of the balance sheet will be $124,500.]

### 15

On the information given below, make a six-column statement, close the ledger, divide profits equally between partners, and show the balance sheet.

*Ledger balances*

| | |
|---|---|
| Proprietor A | $57,000 |
| Proprietor B | 25,000 |
| Bills Payable | 19,000 |
| Bills Receivable | 27,000 |
| Customers | 20,000 |
| Creditors | 25,000 |
| Real Estate | 45,000 |
| Mdse., credit | 4,000 |
| Commission, credit | 3,000 |
| Interest, debit | 1,000 |
| Wages, debit | 35,000 |
| Expense | 5,000 |

*Additional facts*

| | |
|---|---|
| Real estate valuation .................. | $44,500 |
| Mdse., valuation......................... | 51,000 |
| Commission accrued against firm ........ | 1,000 |
| Interest accrued in favor of firm ......... | 500 |
| Wages accrued against firm ............ | 500 |
| Expense (taxes) accrued ................ | 500 |

[The total of the balance sheet should be $143,000.]

## 16

Certain accounts on a trial balance are as follows:

| | | |
|---|---|---|
| Interest .............. | $500 | |
| Commission .......... | | $1,300 |
| Wages ............... | 13,500 | |
| Insurance ............ | 300 | |
| Rent .................. | | 600 |
| Stationery ........... | 400 | |
| Taxes ................ | 200 | |
| Sales .................. | | 140,000 |
| Purchases ............ | 100,000 | |
| Depreciation .......... | 6,000 | |
| Advertising ........... | 1,000 | |

The inventory of merchandise at the beginning of the year was $20,000 (not included in the purchases above), and it is now $25,000. When the books were last closed the proprietor had a credit of $50,000, but nothing has been invested or withdrawn by him since that time. If the books were now to be closed, assuming that the correct figures for all nominal accounts have been given above, how should you show on the proprietor's account his present credit ?

[The proprietor's credit is actually $75,000.]

## 17

In closing books at the end of a year what allowance, if any, should be made for interest and for discount on each of the notes below? Assume notes bearing interest to have run two months and others to have two months yet to run, and that the rate of interest to be used is 6 %.

| | | | |
|---|---|---|---|
| Bills receivable | No. 120 | bearing interest | $1,000 |
| Bills receivable | No. 127 | without interest | 2,000 |
| Bills payable | No. 74 | without interest | 3,000 |
| Bills payable | No. 84 | bearing interest | 4,000 |

What is the effect on the balance sheet?
[Net effect — shrinkage of net assets, $20.]

# THE PRINCIPLES OF LABOR-SAVING DEVICES, I

## Special Columns and Special Books

[Chapter VI, pages 57–66]

### 18

Study the following four imaginary pages of books of account, determine what each page represents as a whole, then interpret each item on each page, find any relation that may exist between any item on one page and any item on any other page, post all items that should be posted, and take a trial balance of these items. (Such a trial balance will be abnormal, for it will show peculiar balances of certain accounts; but since it is taken simply as a test of certain isolated entries, it serves its purpose in spite of peculiarities.)

I

| | | | |
|---|---|---|---|
| Proprietor | Investment | | $3,000 |
| J. White | Shipment, 10/3 | | 2,500 |
| Bills Payable | Our note, with interest | | 5,000 |
| Mdse | Cash sales for the day | | 500 |
| Real Estate | House lot, Y St., sold | | 3,000 |
| Cash Dr. | | | $14,000 |
| Balance | | $8,765 | |

II

| | | Freight | Expense | |
|---|---|---|---|---|
| H. Green | Invoice, 9/5 | | | $5,000 |
| Interest | On #54 paid | | | 50 |
| Expense | Stationery bill, S. W. Co. | | $100 | |
| Freight | On Inv. #649 | $50 | | |
| Expense | Cleaning | | 10 | |
| Freight | On Inv. #653 | 25 | | |
| Expense | | | $110 | 110 |
| Freight | | $75 | | 75 |
| Cash Cr. | | | | $5,235 |
| *Balance* | | | | *$8,765* |
| | | | | $14,000 |

III

| | | | |
|---|---|---|---|
| Cash .............................. | | $500 | |
| P. Brown | | | |
| 16 doz. #25 .............. $4^{00}$ | $64 | | |
| 2 " #38 ..............$10^{00}$ | 20 | 84 | |
| G. Grey | | | |
| 20 doz. #15 .............. $7^{00}$ | | 140 | |
| Mdse. Cr. ......................... | | | $724 |

IV

| | | | |
|---|---|---|---|
| H. Black | | | |
| Inv. #76 ...................... | | $275 | |
| B. Dunn | | | |
| Inv. #77 ...................... | | 125 | |
| Mdse. Dr.......................... | | | $400 |

[Sixteen postings required. Total of trial balance of ledger balances, $14,224.]

19

The following is a page of a book:

| | | | | | | |
|---|---|---|---|---|---|---|
| Jan. 1 | | Balance ...... | .................... | $1,547.30 | | |
| | | A. Andrews .. | His invoice, Dec. 1 .. | .... | .... | $615.10 |
| | | Bills Receivable | No. 127 paid ........ | .... | $500.00 | |
| | | Bills Payable .. | No. 19 discounted.... | .... | .... | 1,000.00 |
| | | Merchandise .. | Cash sales .......... | .... | .... | 173.28 |
| " 2 | | Bills Receivable | No. 116 paid ........ | .... | 123.50 | |
| | | Insurance .... | Premium ret'd on policy | .... | .... | 73.23 |
| " 3 | | Bills Receivable | No. 139 paid ........ | .... | 312.26 | |
| | | Bills Receivable | .................... | .... | $935.76 | 935.76 |
| | | Cash, Dr. .... | .................... | 2,797.37 | .... | $2,797.37 |
| | | | | $4,344.67 | | |

Note fully what transactions are here recorded. What postings should be made, and to which side of each account? If any figures are not to be posted, why not?

[Six postings, or five? Total amount to be posted, $5,421.46, or $5,594.74?]

## 20

Enter the following transactions in the proper books, post, and take a trial balance.

May 1. Begin a general grocery business today, investing cash, $4,000.

May 2. Pay store rent in cash, one month, $60.

May 3. Buy for cash, 200 bu. potatoes @ $.80; 400 lbs. butter @ $.25.

May 4. Buy of John Randolph, on account, 60 bbls. flour @ $4; 20 bbls. salt @ $1.50; 175 lbs. lard @ $.10.

May 5. Sell Alexander Hamilton for cash, 10 bbls. flour @ $4.50; 45 bu. potatoes @ $.80; 2 bbls. salt @ $1.75.

May 6. Sell Benjamin Harrison, on account, 100 lbs. lard @ $.12; 110 lbs. butter @ $.30; 10 bbls. flour at $4.50.

May 8. Buy for cash a set of books for office use, $15.

May 9. Pay John Randolph cash, on account, $56.40.

May 10. Receive cash of Benjamin Harrison, on account, $50.

May 11. Buy of James Otis, on account, 5 bbls. flour @ $3.50; 600 lbs. of lard @ $.08; 500 lbs. butter at $.20; 250 bu. potatoes @ $.70.

May 12. Sell John Hancock, on account, 12 bbls. flour @ $4; 100 lbs. lard @ $.10; 100 lbs. butter @ $.22.

May 13. Sell Benjamin Harrison, on account, 70 bu. potatoes @ $.75; 6 bbls. salt @ $1.70; 100 lbs. lard @ $.12.

May 15. Receive cash of John Hancock, on account, $52.50; pay James Otis cash, on account, $195.

May 16. Buy of John Randolph, on account, 40 bbls. flour @ $3.50.

May 17. Sell Benjamin Harrison, on account, 16 bbls. flour @ $4; 100 lbs. lard @ $.11.

May 18. Give John Randolph your note for goods bought on the 16th; sell Robert Morris for cash, 20 bbls. flour @ $4.10; 212 lbs. butter @ $.20; 60 bu. potatoes @ $.77.

May 20. Sell John Hancock, on account, 10 bbls. flour @ $3.98; 100 lbs. lard @ $.11; 100 lbs. butter @ $.20; 10 bbls. salt @ $1.68.

May 22. Sell George Clinton for cash, 100 lbs. lard @ $.10; sell for cash, 20 bu. potatoes @ $.75.

May 26. John Hancock settles his bill of the 20th; pay your note in favor of John Randolph.

May 28. Pay clerk for one month, cash, $40.

[The entries to the receipts side of the cash book should amount to $4,470.20; to the disbursements side, $766.40; to the sales book, $687.40; to the purchase book, $1,028; to the journal, $140. The trial balance of ledger balances gives a total of $4,464.20.]

## THE PRINCIPLES OF LABOR-SAVING DEVICES, II

### Controlling Accounts and Discounts

[Chapter VI, pages 66–80]

### 21

Enter the following transactions in a journal, a sales book, a special-column cash book (all expenses to be carried to one expense account), post to a sales ledger and a general ledger, and take a trial balance.

The proprietor invests $15,000 worth of merchandise and $5,000 in cash.

Rent is paid, $300; postage, $20; stationery, $50.

Goods are sold to Brown for $1,000, to Gray for $800, to White for $2,000, to cash customers for $1,500.

Wages are paid, $200.

Cash is received from Brown, $1,000; from Gray, $800; from White, $1,000.

The proprietor draws $100 for his personal use.

[The total number of postings to the general ledger, including cash, is ten, — two from the journal, six from the cash book, two from the sales book. The total of the trial balance of ledger balances is $19,900.]

### 22

The following transactions are to be entered in complete form, with full details and index references; the resulting figures are to be carried through a six-column statement; the books are then to be closed as for the end of a year, and a balance sheet for the beginning of the new year is to be shown.

The books to be used are a journal, a special-column cash book, a sales book, a purchase book, a sales ledger, a purchase ledger, and a general ledger. When insufficient details for a complete record of sale or other entry are given below, reasonable details are to be assumed. Six per cent should be used for interest and discount.

The closing inventory of merchandise is $35,000. In determining and recording profit, care should be taken that all necessary additional facts are considered.

Ethan Allen, Ambrose Burnside, and George Custer form a partnership (A. B. C. Co.) on January 1, and take over the assets and liabilities of the business of Ethan Allen, who is given credit for the net assets of his business as shown by his books. Ambrose Burnside contributes $20,000 worth of merchandise, and George Custer contributes a note of George Thomas, face $20,000, dated January 1, running four months with interest. The partnership agreement provides monthly salaries for partners as follows: Ethan Allen, $1,000; Ambrose Burnside, $500; and George Custer, $300. It provides that 5% interest shall be credited to each partner on his capital investment. Profits, after partners' salaries and interest have been provided for, shall be divided equally.

On January 1, the books of Ethan Allen's business show the following items: Building, $100,000; Equipment, $2,000; Accounts Receivable, $4,900 (Philip Sheridan, $3,400, due January 20; Horatio Gates, $1,500, due January 10); Bills Receivable, $13,500 (William Sherman, $4,000, dated December 15, one month; Thomas Jackson, $6,500, dated December 1, two months; Robert Lee, $3,000, dated November 1, payable on demand with interest); Merchandise (on hand), $11,000; Cash, $5,330; Office Supplies (on hand), $274; Insurance (prepaid to July 1), $800; Accounts Payable, $5,000 (Anthony Wayne, $5,000, due January 8); Bills Payable, $8,000 (No. 1, $4,000, dated September 25, four months with interest; No. 2, $4,000, dated December 2, sixty days); Allowance for Bad Debts, $1,000; Taxes (accrued against the business), $1,800. Open the books of the new business, show a balance sheet for its beginning, and then enter the later transactions.

Jan. 1. The accrued taxes are paid.

Jan. 2. Goods are sold to Ulysses Grant, cash, $3,000. Bill for three months' supply of coal is paid, $300.

Jan. 3. Goods are bought of John Stark, payment due in 15 days, $7,850.

Jan. 4. Goods are bought of Robert Anderson, cash, $2,000.

Jan. 5. Telephone bill is paid, three months in advance, $21. A motor truck is bought, cash, $2,900, and freight is paid on it, $125.

Jan. 6. Wages are paid: bookkeeper, $30; clerk, $12; driver, $26. Goods are sold to George McClellan, $1,000, — $400 cash down, balance 10 days.

Jan. 8. Announcements of the new partnership are sent to customers and $35 is paid for printing them. Anthony Wayne accepts merchandise in settlement of the amount owed him.

Jan. 9. John Stark's draft on A. B. C. Co. is accepted, payable in nine days, for the amount of the bill due him.

Jan. 10. Horatio Gates pays his bill. Goods are sold to John Pope, cash, $900.

Jan. 11. A note signed by the A. B. C. Co. is discounted at a bank, face $20,000, 30 days. Goods are bought of George Thomas, cash, $18,000.

Jan. 12. Robert Lee pays his note. A subscription for charity is paid, $225.

Jan. 13. Wages are paid at the same rate as on the 6th. Insurance premium on stock of goods is paid for one year, $300.

Jan. 15. William Sherman pays his note. Thomas Jackson's note is discounted at a bank.

Jan. 16. Goods are sold for cash, $400. George McClellan pays the balance of his bill.

Jan. 17. Freight is paid, $164. Goods are sold to Horatio Gates, $15,000, 30 days.

Jan. 18. The acceptance of the 9th is paid. Goods are sold to John Fremont, $12,000, 15 days.

Jan. 19. Money is borrowed on a note of A. B. C. Co., $7,000, 90 days, bearing interest.

Jan. 20. Philip Sheridan pays his bill. Wages are paid as before.

Jan. 22. Goods are bought of Robert Anderson, $10,000, 10 days.

Jan. 23. Postage is paid, $25. Ambrose Burnside draws for his own use, $250.

Jan. 24. A carpenter's bill for remodeling offices is paid, $600. One of the remodeled offices is rented, and two months' rent is received in advance, $80.

Jan. 25. Ethan Allen pays a private bill out of the cash drawer, $40. Note No. 1 is paid.

Jan. 26. Goods are sold to Winfield Scott, $9,000, 10 days.

Jan. 27. A draft on Horatio Gates is drawn — payable in 20 days, to the order of A. B. C. Co. — for the amount of his bill. Wages are paid as before.

Jan. 29. The draft drawn on the 27th is returned accepted. Electric light bill is paid, $20.

Jan. 30. Horatio Gates's acceptance of the draft is discounted at a bank. Goods are bought of Henry Slocum, $5,000, 15 days, and a 15-day note of A. B. C. Co. is given in payment.

Jan. 31. Note No. 2 is paid.

[This problem is meant to give wide latitude to the student in method of entry and in valuing assets at the end of the period. So no exact cue to acceptable answers is given.]

## 23

The following transactions are to be carried through the ledger, the books are to be closed, and the six-column statement and the balance sheet as of June 1 are to be shown. The books to be used are a journal, a sales book, a purchase book, a special-column cash book, and the necessary ledgers. Commercial discounts are regularly as follows: 10 days, 6 %; 30 days, 5 %; 60 days, net. Interest is to be figured at 6 %.

May 1. You begin business, as sole proprietor, under the name of The Kensington Company. You buy a stock of merchandise for $10,000. You give in part payment notes which you hold as follows: Charles Darwin, $3,000, dated April 15, payable in one month; Herbert Spencer, $1,000, dated today, payable in two months, bearing interest; Louis Pasteur, $1,000, dated April 1, payable in 30 days. The balance you pay in cash, and the rest of your original cash capital of $7,000 you turn in to the business. The notes and the cash constitute your investment in the business. Pay rent up to July 1, $60.

May 2. Sell goods to Robert Boyle (usual discounts), $525. Pay bill of $50, half of which is for bookkeeping books and half for printing advertising flyers.

May 3. Pay cartage bill for removal of your stock of goods to your store, $53.50. Sells goods to Evangelista Torricelli, ten days net, $775. Sell merchandise (30 days net) to Friedrich von Humboldt for his note for 30 days, $2,500.

May 4. Sell goods to Thomas Huxley (usual discounts), $1,750. Pay express bill, $10. Buy merchandise of Samuel F. B. Morse (usual discounts), $500.

May 5. Buy for cash a store sign, $20. Buy goods of Benjamin Franklin (usual discounts), $250. Discount your own note (signed by The Kensington Company) for $750 dated today, payable in 30 days.

May 8. Pay wages to two clerks at $10 each. Receive from legacy of Galileo Galilei, $2,000, which you invest in the business. Pay for temporary decorations during a festival week, $50.

May 12. Torricelli pays his bill. Pay S. F. B. Morse.

May 14. Thomas Huxley pays his bill. Sell goods to Isaac Newton, 10 days net, $2,750. Sell goods to Hermann Helmholz (usual discounts), $7,500.

May 15. Pay wages as before.

May 16. Discount Humboldt's note.

May 21. Draw a draft on Isaac Newton payable in three days, for the amount of his bill of the 14th. Buy a new suit for yourself, $40, and pay for it out of the cash drawer.

May 22. Newton accepts the draft you drew on him on the 21st.

May 24. Newton pays his draft.

May 29. Pay wages as before, two weeks.

May 31. Robert Boyle pays his bill. Pay Franklin his bill.

The inventory of merchandise is now found to be $1,500; wages due amount to $7.50; equipment and supplies are thought to be worth $40; no other allowances are deemed to be necessary.

[The balance of the cash book is $11,829.92; the total of the purchase book is $10,750; the total of the sales book is $15,800. The total of the balance sheet is $20,869.92.]

## 24

The following transactions are to be entered in complete form, with full details and index references; the resulting figures are to be carried through a six-column statement; the books are then to be closed as for the end of a year, and a balance sheet for the beginning of the new year is to be shown.

The books to be used are a journal, a special-column cash book, a sales book, a purchase book, a sales ledger, a purchase ledger, and a general ledger. When insufficient details for a complete record of sale or other entry are given below, reasonable details are to be assumed. On all goods bought or sold, 3% cash discount is allowed when payment is made within ten days. Six per cent should be used for interest.

The closing inventory of merchandise is $48,353.10, and of stationery $200. In determining and recording profit, care should be taken that all necessary additional facts are considered.

U. S. Grant begins a business as the "Granting Company" on July 1, 1914, with the following capital: building at 369 Pleasant street valued at $30,000; cash, $30,000; a promissory note of W. S. Hancock (B.R. #1), for $2,000, dated July 1, 1914, payable in two months; a promissory note of G. G. Meade (B.R. #2), for $4,000, dated June 1, 1914, payable in two months; a promissory note of P. G. T. Beauregard (B.R. #3), for $1,000, dated June 16, 1914, payable in one month; a promissory note of W. T. Sherman (B.R. #4), for $3,000, dated May 1, 1914, payable on demand with interest. The company employs a bookkeeper at $30 per week, an assistant bookkeeper at $20, three clerks at $12 each, a driver at $24, a buyer at $42, and an office boy at $8. Following are the transactions of the business: —

July 1. Office furniture is bought and paid for, $1,000; office books, stationery and printing, ink, etc., $250; stamps and stamped envelopes, $30.

July 2. Goods are bought of W. S. Rosecrans, $8,000; of J. Hooker, cash, $6,000.

July 3. A second-hand motor truck in perfect condition is bought at a bankruptcy sale, cash, $1,000, and freight is paid on it, $130. Telephones are installed and three months' charges are paid in advance, $50. A contract is made with a daily paper to publish the advertisements of the new business for $60 a month, payable in advance. The first month's payment is made.

July 5. P. H. Sheridan buys goods, $1,400. Goods are bought of A. E. Burnside, cash, $12,000.

July 6. Wages are paid.

July 8. Goods are bought of J. Longstreet, $14,000.

July 9. A draft drawn on the Granting Company by W. S. Rosecrans, payable in three days, for the amount of its bill, is accepted (B.P. #1).

July 10. A note signed by the Granting Company is discounted at the Merchants' Bank, face $10,000, 30 days (B.P. #2). W. T. Sherman pays his note (B.R. #4).

July 11. Goods are bought of G. G. Meade, cash, $12,000.

July 12. The promissory note of G. G. Meade (B.R. #2) is discounted at the Merchants' Bank. The acceptance of July 9 is paid.

July 13. Wages are paid. Goods are sold to G. B. McClellan, $1,150.

July 15. J. E. Johnston buys goods, $400.

July 16. P. G. T. Beauregard pays his promissory note due today (B.R. #3). J. Longstreet buys goods, $1,200, and gives his note payable in 30 days (B.R. #5).

July 17. Goods are sold to T. J. Jackson, cash, $600.

July 18. Money is borrowed on a note of the Granting Company for $8,000, 30 days, with interest (B.P. #3). J. Longstreet is paid.

July 19. Insurance premium on the stock of goods is paid for one year, $200, policy #64,510.

July 20. Wages are paid.

July 22. The Uwantus Building Company is paid for remodeling the offices, $600. One of the remodeled offices is rented and three months' rent is received in advance, $200.

July 23. G. B. McClellan pays his bill. The winter's supply of coal is paid for, $200.

July 24. A donation to the Red Cross is made, $200. Goods are sold for cash, $2,400.

July 25. A draft on P. H. Sheridan is drawn, payable in 10 days, to the order of the Granting Company for the amount of his bill. A bill of the Model Company, for goods bought by Mrs. Grant, is paid, $150. J. E. Johnston pays his bill of the 15th.

July 26. The draft drawn on the 25th is returned accepted.

July 27. P. H. Sheridan's acceptance of the draft of the 25th is discounted at the Merchants' Bank. Wages are paid.

July 29. Mr. Grant draws for his own use, $300.

July 30. Goods are bought of W. S. Rosecrans, $2,000.

July 31. Goods are sold to G. B. McClellan, $1,000; and to J. E. Johnston, $1,000, — $450 cash paid, balance, 30 days.

[This problem is meant to give the student latitude of method in treating interest, discounts, allowances, etc., and therefore no definite figures are given as a cue to correct answers. It may be worth his while to attempt the handling of dummy documents, cash, merchandise, etc., and then see whether his papers at the close show that his situation is what it is represented by the books to be.]

## BALANCE SHEET AND INCOME SHEET

[Chapter VII]

### 25

The annual report of a corporation shows the following figures: Undivided Profits, credit balance at the beginning of the year, $20,000; Merchandise, profit, $150,000; Expense, $100,000; Dividends, declared but not paid, $50,000; Permanent Surplus, increased $15,000. Present the Profit and Loss account for the year.

[The balance sheet shows a credit balance to Undivided Profits, $5,000.]

### 26

Schedule I was the balance sheet at the beginning of the year. Schedule II is the trial balance at the end of the year before the books are closed. There are no outstanding or accrued items, and no inventories. Give the balance sheet at the close of the year and test it by an income sheet.

I

| | | | |
|---|---|---|---|
| Real Estate | $10,000 | Proprietor | $45,000 |
| Mdse. | 25,000 | Bills Payable | 5,000 |
| Bills Rec. | 8,000 | Accts. Pay. | 12,000 |
| Accts. Rec. | 12,000 | Accrued Liabilities | 610 |
| Cash | 7,610 | | |
| | $62,610 | | $62,610 |

II

| | | |
|---|---|---|
| Proprietor | | $43,000 |
| Bills Payable | | 4,000 |
| Accounts Payable | | 10,000 |
| Real Estate | $41,350 | |
| Bills Receivable | 6,400 | |
| Cash | 1,516 | |
| Repairs | 88 | |
| Freight | 249 | |
| Insurance | 250 | |
| Expense | 2,740 | |
| Purchases | 64,550 | |
| Sales | | 67,167 |
| Interest | | 740 |
| Commission | | 236 |
| Accounts Receivable | 8,000 | |
| | $125,143 | $125,143 |

Why has the proprietor's balance shrunk ?

## 27

Below is a trial balance taken before the books were closed, an income sheet, and a balance sheet. Show (*a*) the ledger as it looked before closing [totals or balances only], (*b*) the closing items, and (*c*) the ledger as it looked after closing.

| | | |
|---|---|---|
| Proprietor | | $140,000 |
| Bills Payable | $20,000 | 30,000 |
| Accounts Payable | 310,000 | 328,000 |
| Merchandise | 450,000 | 350,000 |
| Accounts Receivable | 375,000 | 353,000 |
| Fixtures | 4,000 | |
| Cash | 6,700 | |
| Wages | 20,000 | |
| Insurance | 400 | |
| Taxes | 2,000 | |
| Rent | 5,000 | |
| Interest | 800 | 100 |
| General Expense | 7,200 | |
| | $1,201,100 | $1,201,100 |

| | | |
|---|---|---|
| Mdse. sales | | $350,000 |
| Mdse. inventory, 1911 | $150,000 | |
| Mdse. purchases | 300,000 | |
| Mdse. handled | $450,000 | |
| Mdse. inventory, 1912 | 140,000 | |
| Mdse. cost of sales | | 310,000 |
| Gross profit | | $40,000 |
| Wages | $20,500 | |
| Insurance | 200 | |
| Taxes | 2,000 | |
| Rent | 5,000 | |
| Interest | 600 | |
| General Expense | 6,700 | 35,000 |
| Net income | | $5,000 |

| | | | |
|---|---|---|---|
| Merchandise | $140,000 | Proprietor | $145,000 |
| Accounts Rec. | 22,000 | Bills Payable | 10,000 |
| Fixtures | 4,000 | Accounts Pay. | 18,000 |
| Cash | 6,700 | Wages Accrued | 500 |
| Supplies | 500 | | |
| Prepaid insurance | 200 | | |
| Prepaid interest | 100 | | |
| | $173,500 | | $173,500 |

[The work should be self-proving.]

## 28

You are ordered by a court to close the affairs of an illegal corporation. The following is the trial balance as you find it:

| | | |
|---|---|---|
| Capital stock | | $169,000 |
| Real Estate | $70,000 | |
| Mortgages Payable | | 55,000 |
| Bills Payable | | 25,000 |
| Bills Receivable | 15,000 | |
| Accounts Receivable | 17,000 | |
| Merchandise | 150,000 | |
| Cash | 7,000 | |
| Expenses | 15,000 | |
| Interest | 3,000 | |
| Taxes | 2,500 | |
| Sales | | 30,500 |
| | $279,500 | $279,500 |

You dispose of the real estate at 90% of the book valuation; you collect 75% of the accounts receivable; you get $130,000 for the merchandise; the other assets realize 100%. Determine surplus or deficit and explain, in the form of a Profit and Loss account, its origin. Prove your figures by a balance sheet after all other assets have been converted into cash but before any debts have been paid.

How is the Merchandise account kept in these books?

[Figure of surplus or deficit, $21,250.]

## 29

The following items appear in the report of a corporation. Put them in the form of a balance sheet and an income sheet, and arrange the latter so as to give the clearest view of the operations of the business.

| | | | |
|---|---|---|---|
| Sales | $249,000 | Wages paid | $83,000 |
| Accounts receivable | 17,000 | Dividends paid | 9,000 |
| Material on hand | 14,000 | Bonds issued | 30,000 |
| Capital stock | 90,000 | Real estate | 25,000 |
| Wages due | 7,000 | Cash | 12,000 |

| | | | |
|---|---|---|---|
| Patent rights | $16,000 | Rentals earned and received | $200 |
| Depreciation | 3,000 | Rentals earned but not due | 300 |
| Bills receivable | 7,000 | Accounts payable | 46,000 |
| Interest paid | 900 | Repairs of plant | 6,000 |
| Interest accrued to pay | 600 | Surplus for the year | 14,000 |
| Surplus a year ago | 48,100 | Miscellaneous costs | 11,500 |
| Insurance paid | 500 | Material purchased | 85,000 |
| Insurance unexpired | 200 | Selling costs | 20,000 |
| Material on hand a year ago | 21,600 | Estimated present value of outstanding advertising paid for | 2,000 |
| Taxes paid | 800 | Loss by defalcation | 10,000 |
| Taxes accrued to pay | 800 | | |
| Plant | 66,000 | | |
| Merchandise | 67,000 | | |

[The ultimate results should be self-proving.]

## 30

The trial balance of a business is given as below:

| | | |
|---|---|---|
| 1. Capital Stock | | $193,000 |
| 2. Real Estate | $50,000 | |
| 3. Accounts Receivable | 60,000 | |
| 4. Merchandise Inventory (beginning) | 50,000 | |
| 5. Raw Material | 56,000 | |
| 6. Plant | 75,000 | |
| 7. Cash | 15,000 | |
| 8. Surplus (beginning) | | 34,000 |
| 9. Wages and Salaries | 153,000 | |
| 10. Advertising | 5,000 | |
| 11. Insurance | 1,000 | |
| 12. General Expenses | 15,000 | |
| 13. Rent of Real Estate Let | | 2,000 |
| 14. Fire Loss | 5,000 | |
| 15. Sales | | 256,000 |
| | $485,000 | $485,000 |

On examination of the books and the establishment, certain other facts are disclosed about items on the trial balance, as follows:

Item 2 comprises $20,000 worth of property let and $30,000 worth occupied.

Item 4 has an inventory of $60,000.

Item 5 has an inventory of $18,000.

Item 6 is worth $73,000.

Item 9 includes $2,000 of unearned salaries paid while the business was shut down after a fire, $3,000 spent for work installing a water system for the buildings, and $15,000 for salaries of salesmen.

Item 10 includes $1,000 spent for preparation of material and plates not yet used but about to be used.

Item 11 includes $200 on real estate let, $400 on plant and real estate occupied, $400 on merchandise.

Item 12 includes $10,000 for selling costs and $5,000 for manufacturing costs.

The directors now declare 20% dividends; but these dividends are not yet paid.

Show the income sheet in what seems to you the best form for this business, and show the balance sheet after the declaration of dividends.

[Surplus for the year, $21,400; Surplus on the balance sheet $48,400; assets, $280,000.]

## DEPRECIATION AND RESERVES

[Chapter VIII]

### 31

The following is a condensed trial balance of a partnership. The only inventory is for supplies, which amounts to $25,000. No accrued or prepaid items are outstanding. Allow 10% depreciation on all accounts (except cash and supplies) representing property, 5% on all sums due the business from outside, credit the partners 5% interest on their investments, credit salaries to the partners at $3,000 for A and $2,000 for B, and then divide profit or loss equally between the partners. Show the balance sheet ready for the next year.

| | | |
|---|---|---|
| A | | $40,000 |
| B | | 20,000 |
| Plant and Machinery | $45,000 | |
| Supplies | 43,000 | |
| Sales | | 95,000 |
| Labor | 30,000 | |
| Expense | 7,800 | |
| Interest | 600 | |
| Discounts | 1,250 | |
| Fuel | 3,000 | |
| Insurance | 1,150 | |
| Freight | 1,500 | |
| Accounts Payable | | 9,000 |
| Accounts Receivable | 32,000 | |
| Steam Earnings | | 1,500 |
| Cash | 200 | |
| | $165,500 | $165,500 |

[Balance sheet totals, $97,700.]

### 32

You are given the following trial balance, dated February 29, and are told that all transactions have been entered, but the books have not been closed since January 1.

| | | |
|---|---|---|
| Capital Stock | | $93,750 |
| Plant, etc. | $70,675 | |
| Bills Receivable | 38,400 | |
| Accounts Receivable | 22,500 | |
| Cash | 14,065 | |
| Bills Payable | | 37,500 |
| Accounts Payable | | 6,250 |
| Sales | | 80,250 |
| Wages and Salaries | 24,592 | |
| Raw Material | 37,908 | |
| Merchandise Discounts | 440 | 2,500 |
| Power, etc. | 3,125 | |
| Insurance | 155 | |
| Taxes | 310 | |
| Interest | 410 | |
| Commission | 1,875 | |
| Office Supplies | 180 | |
| Sundry Expense | 4,505 | |
| Repairs | 685 | |
| Depreciation | 425 | |
| | $220,250 | $220,250 |

The business was reorganized on March 1, and in preparation for the entries for the new business the books were closed for the old. The resulting balance sheet is shown below.

| | | | |
|---|---|---|---|
| Plant, etc. | $70,675 | Capital Stock | $93,750 |
| Bills Receivable | 38,400 | Bills Payable | 37,500 |
| Accounts Receivable | 22,500 | Accounts Payable | 6,250 |
| Cash | 14,065 | Wages Accrued | 785 |
| Raw Material | 15,400 | Interest Accrued | 155 |
| Insurance Prepaid | 100 | Allowance for Bad Debts | 1,200 |
| Office Supplies | 80 | Reserve for Deprec'on | 3,000 |
| | | Undivided Profits | 18,580 |
| | $161,220 | | $161,220 |

Show the income sheet.

[The work should be self-proving.]

## 33

A business presents the following condensed income sheet and condensed balance sheet.

Jan. 1, 1914 — Dec. 31, 1914

| | |
|---|---|
| Merchandise credit balance | $150,000 |
| General expenses | 130,000 |
| | $20,000 |
| Maintenance | 10,000 |
| Net profit | $10,000 |
| Dividends | 9,000 |
| Surplus for the year | $1,000 |

January 1, 1915

| | | | |
|---|---|---|---|
| Plant | $100,000 | Capital Stock | $150,000 |
| Supplies | 10,000 | Payables | 10,000 |
| Receivables | 45,000 | Surplus | 5,000 |
| Cash | 10,000 | | |
| | $165,000 | | $165,000 |

Assume, therefore, that wear and tear requires an annual maintenance charge of $10,000. Show the income sheet and the balance sheet as they would have looked if each of the policies indicated below, taken in turn and not cumulatively, had been substituted for the policy which resulted in the figures above, assuming that in all respects not specified the policy was unchanged. [The most convenient way to make such a comparative study is to provide a column for all titles, both income sheet and balance sheet one under the other, leaving spaces for new titles, and six columns for figures, and, after writing in the first column the figures given above, give substituted figures for the other policies in the succeeding columns.]

(*a*) Spending only $5,000 for maintenance.

(*b*) Spending only $5,000 for maintenance, but paying $14,000 in dividends.

(*c*) Spending nothing for maintenance, and declaring but not yet paying dividends of $9,000.

(*d*) Spending $10,000 for maintenance, paying $5,000 for dividends, and setting aside a $5,000 reserve for depreciation.

(*e*) Spending $5,000 for maintenance, establishing a special cash maintenance fund of $5,000, and declaring but not yet paying a $9,000 dividend.

[The work should be self-proving. The balance-sheet figures of Surplus for the substitutions run as follows: $5,000, nil, $5,000, $4,000, $5,000.]

## 34

A condensed tentative balance sheet, with $10,000 net income for the year on the tentative income sheet before any account is taken of depreciation, reads as follows:

| | | | |
|---|---|---|---|
| Plant, etc. .......... | $80,000 | Capital Stock ....... | $100,000 |
| Receivables ........ | 40,000 | Payables ........... | 40,000 |
| Merchandise ....... | 33,000 | Surplus ............. | 10,000 |
| Cash .............. | 7,000 | Undivided Profits .... | 10,000 |
| | $160,000 | | $160,000 |

The directors are divided in opinion on a policy to adopt regarding depreciation and dividends. Show the balance sheet as it would look after the adoption of each of the following policies, supposing the tentative sheet above embodies no provision for either depreciation or dividends. Find the surplus for the year, — i. e., the net income not distributed to those entitled to profits.

(*a*) Accepting the theory that depreciation has actually occurred in the last year to the amount of $5,000, and declaring (but not yet paying) a dividend of 6 %.

(*b*) Accepting the theory that maintenance has kept up the property, but setting aside a reserve of $6,000, to make assurance doubly sure, for depreciation, and declaring a dividend of 5 %.

(*c*) Discovering that depreciation had been going on for some years up till a year ago and, though the plant has been maintained for the last year at the standard of a year ago, the total depreciation not recorded on the books is $15,000; but, on the ground that the shrinkage will be immediately made good, refusing to write off the item of Plant; and declaring a dividend of 3 %.

[Surplus on the balance sheet, $9,000, $9,000, $2,000. Surplus for the year, −$1,000, $5,000, $7,000.]

## INTERPRETATION OF BALANCE SHEETS

[Chapter IX]

### 35

Should you be inclined to recommend an investment in this business or a loan to it ?

*Balance sheets, dated Dec. 31*

| | 1910 | 1911 | 1912 |
|---|---|---|---|
| Real Estate ..... | $100,000 | $100,000 | $100,000 |
| Mdse. ........... | 100,000 | 125,000 | 150,000 |
| Bills Rec. ........ | 50,000 | 50,000 | 60,000 |
| Accts. Rec. ....... | 40,000 | 50,000 | 60,000 |
| Fittings ......... | 5,000 | 5,000 | 5,000 |
| Cash ........... | 12,000 | 13,000 | 14,000 |
| | $307,000 | $343,000 | $389,000 |
| Capital Stock .... | $200,000 | $200,000 | $200,000 |
| Bills Payable .... | 15,000 | 20,000 | 25,000 |
| Accts. Pay. ....... | 67,000 | 93,000 | 129,000 |
| Surplus ......... | 25,000 | 30,000 | 35,000 |
| | $307,000 | $343,000 | $389,000 |

*Other figures*

| | 1910 | 1911 | 1912 |
|---|---|---|---|
| Purchases ....... | $600,000 | $700,000 | $800,000 |
| Sales ........... | 700,000 | 825,000 | 1,000,000 |
| Discounts taken .. | 30,000 | 35,000 | 40,000 |
| Discounts given .. | 25,000 | 36,000 | 50,000 |
| Dividends paid .. | 6 % | 7 % | 8 % |

[Suggestions toward an answer: — analysis and computation from the figures shown gives the total of a where-got-gone statement for the two years as $82,000; percentage of discounts taken on all purchases paid for in the second year as 5.2 %; expenses in the second year as $130,000.]

## 36

The balance sheet of a corporation on January 1, 1914, stood as follows:

| | | | |
|---|---|---|---|
| Real Estate | $50,000 | Capital Stock | $200,000 |
| Plant | 95,000 | Accounts Payable | 20,000 |
| Horses, etc. | 15,000 | Bills Payable | 25,000 |
| Patents | 20,000 | Profit and Loss | 15,000 |
| Merchandise | 30,000 | | |
| Accounts Receivable | 30,000 | | |
| Cash | 20,000 | | |
| | $260,000 | | $260,000 |

On January 1, 1915, the books showed the following:

| | | | |
|---|---|---|---|
| Real Estate | $55,000 | Capital Stock | $200,000 |
| Plant | 88,000 | Accounts Payable | 12,000 |
| Horses, etc. | 12,000 | Bills Payable | 17,000 |
| Patents | 19,000 | Profit and Loss | 33,000 |
| Merchandise | 42,000 | | |
| Accounts Receivable | 28,000 | | |
| Cash | 18,000 | | |
| | $262,000 | | $262,000 |

Show in tabular form what has become of the profits earned.
Should you recommend that a dividend be declared ?
[" Where-got-gone " totals, $33,000.]

## 37

Assume that valuations are conservative in the business presenting the following figures.

Should you be inclined to recommend investment in this business or a loan to it ? Is the surplus real or fictitious ?

Resources

| *Dec. 31* | *1909* | *1910* | *1911* |
|---|---|---|---|
| Real Estate | $100,000 | $125,000 | $150,000 |
| Mdse. | 100,000 | 100,000 | 100,000 |
| Bills Receivable | 25,000 | 20,000 | 15,000 |
| Accts. Receivable | 30,000 | 25,000 | 20,000 |
| Fittings | 5,000 | 4,000 | 3,000 |
| Cash | 15,000 | 17,000 | 15,000 |
| | $275,000 | $291,000 | $303,000 |

LIABILITIES

| *Dec. 31* | *1909* | *1910* | *1911* |
|---|---|---|---|
| Capital Stock .... | $200,000 | $200,000 | $200,000 |
| Bills Payable .... | 40,000 | 42,000 | 35,000 |
| Accts. Payable ... | 15,000 | 27,000 | 21,000 |
| Surplus ......... | 20,000 | 22,000 | 47,000 |
| | $275,000 | $291,000 | $303,000 |

ADDITIONAL FIGURES

| *Year* | *1909* | *1910* | *1911* |
|---|---|---|---|
| Purchases ....... | $300,000 | $325,000 | $350,000 |
| Sales ............ | 325,000 | 350,000 | 400,000 |
| Discounts given .. | 16,000 | 17,000 | 20,000 |
| Discounts taken .. | 15,000 | 15,100 | 15,200 |
| Dividends ....... | 6% | 6% | 6% |

## 38

A balance sheet for January 1, 1913, was as follows:

| | | | |
|---|---|---|---|
| Real Estate ........ | $75,000 | Capital Stock ..... | $200,000 |
| Notes Receivable ... | 15,000 | Notes Payable .... | 75,000 |
| Accts. Receivable ... | 125,000 | Accts. Payable .... | 50,000 |
| Mdse. ............. | 118,000 | Surplus ........... | 25,000 |
| Cash .............. | 17,000 | | |
| | $350,000 | | $350,000 |

The business of the year following may be summarized as follows: merchandise bought, $100,000, and paid for merchandise bought, $100,000; merchandise sold, $160,000, and collected on merchandise sold, $145,000; expenses paid, $30,000; net profits, $40,000, including dividends paid amounting to $25,000.

Show the balance sheet for Jan. 1, 1914, supposing sales of merchandise to be the only source of profits.

[The trial balance of ledger balances after closing the books will show a total of $365,000.]

## 39

A summary of the transactions of a corporation for one year is as follows: net income, now in the form of cash, $34,000; dividends declared but not yet paid, $25,000; bills payable converted into capital stock, $20,000; real estate bought for cash, $15,000; notes received in payment of outstanding ledger accounts, $7,000; all other transactions have exactly offset each other, so that except for those mentioned above the status is exactly as it was a year ago. The balance sheet at the beginning of the old year was as follows:

| | | | |
|---|---|---|---|
| Real Estate | $70,000 | Capital Stock | $197,000 |
| Machinery | 86,000 | Bills Pay. | 25,000 |
| Bills Rec. | 24,000 | Accts. Pay. | 12,000 |
| Accts. Rec. | 20,000 | Surplus | 21,000 |
| Mdse. | 31,000 | | |
| Cash | 24,000 | | |
| | $255,000 | | $255,000 |

Show the balance sheet for the beginning of the new year. [Totals, $289,000.]

## 40

The following balance sheet was reported for Jan. 1, 1914.

| | | | |
|---|---|---|---|
| Plant | $350,000 | Cap. Stock | $400,000 |
| Bills Rec. | 5,000 | Bills Pay. | 50,000 |
| Accts. Rec. | 80,000 | Accts. Pay. | 40,000 |
| Mdse. | 70,000 | Surplus | 25,000 |
| Cash | 10,000 | | |
| | $515,000 | | $515,000 |

Transactions with the outside business world caused the following changes in real accounts:

| | |
|---|---|
| Cash increase | $7,000 |
| Bills payable decrease | 12,000 |
| Mdse. increase | 11,000 |
| Accts. payable increase | 20,850 |

The following is a copy of the Profit and Loss account on the ledger for 1914:

| | | | | | |
|---|---|---|---|---|---|
| Feb. 1. | Bills Receivable | $200 | Jan. 1. | Balance | $25,000 |
| Dec. 31. | Accts. Receivable | 700 | Dec. 31. | Interest | 400 |
| | Expense | 400 | | Rent | 1,200 |
| | Wages | 28,000 | | Trading | 42,950 |
| | Allowance for Bad Debts | 400 | | | |
| | Depreciation | 7,000 | | | |
| | Dividend No. 67 | 3,500 | | | |
| | Dividend No. 68 | 3,500 | | | |
| | Balance | 25,850 | | | |
| | | $69,550 | | | $69,550 |

Show the income sheet for 1914 and the balance sheet for Jan. 1, 1915.

[Total for balance sheet 1915 is $525,100. Surplus for the year is $850.]

## THE ELEMENTS OF COST ACCOUNTING

[Chapter X]

### 41

What expense and income accounts should you recommend (choose titles that suggest the items to be carried to each account) for a business operating as follows:

Owning its own store building.
Doing its own heating, lighting, elevator service, from its own power plant.
Buying all its goods in its own town.
Doing its own hauling and delivering.
Paying the clerks regular salaries and bonuses for large sales.
Advertising by electric displays, window displays, newspapers, and circulars.
Conducting rest and recreation rooms for employees.
Allowing interest on undrawn salaries.
Investing its surplus in loans to local enterprises.
Selling goods for cash, for credit, and on the installment plan (in the latter case charging higher prices and sending out collectors).

### 42

What should you recommend for ledger accounts in the business indicated below: purchasing for cash farm produce through traveling buyers who take always the full product of a farm — fields, tilled lands, and orchards; doing its own harvesting; sorting such produce into grades at city warehouses; packing the better grades in special packages; selling the better grades, through local and traveling salesmen, at wholesale; selling culls directly at retail; feeding the waste to hogs kept in the suburbs solely for the utilization of that waste; killing, dressing, and selling the pork.

## 43

Suppose that you are engaged in the manufacture of chair stock.

You get some of your raw material by buying sawed lumber, some by buying logs and sawing them, some by buying trees on the stump (you do not buy the land on which they stand) and doing your own logging, shipping, sawing, etc., and some by buying land, getting off the logs, and then selling the land.

Name the ledger accounts that you deem necessary for adequate accounting.

## STATISTICS IN ACCOUNTING

[Chapter XI]

### 44

How far do the other figures explain for the year 1911 the first three items?

| | |
|---|---|
| Receipts from passengers have declined | $50,000 |
| Receipts from freight have declined .. | 100,000 |
| Operating expenses have increased ... | 200,000 |

| | 1910 | 1911 |
|---|---|---|
| Passengers carried ................ | 873,000 | 892,000 |
| Passenger miles ................... | 48,015,000 | 50,865,000 |
| Average number miles per passenger . | 55 | 57 |
| Passenger tariff rates unchanged | | |
| Miles traveled on local tickets ...... | 15,500,000 | 10,355,000 |
| " " " interline tickets ... | 13,400,000 | 14,220,000 |
| " " " mileage tickets ... | 9,100,000 | 10,020,000 |
| " " " season and commutation tickets ..... | 10,015,000 | 16,270,000 |
| Passengers per train mile ........... | 90 | 85 |
| Passengers per car mile ............. | 18 | 16 |
| Tons carried ....................... | 9,000,000 | 10,000,000 |
| Ton miles ......................... | 540,000,000 | 640,000,000 |
| Average miles each ton carried ...... | 60 | 64 |
| Freight tariff rates unchanged | | |
| Tons per train mile ................ | 280 | 265 |
| Tons per car mile .................. | 9 | 8 |
| Company ton miles ................ | 20,000,000 | 70,000,000 |
| Revenue ton miles ................. | 520,000,000 | 570,000,000 |
| Ton miles local traffic .............. | 300,000,000 | 75,000,000 |
| Ton miles interline traffic ........... | 240,000,000 | 565,000,000 |
| Tons of products of agriculture ...... | 2,000,000 | 2,830,000 |
| " " " " forestry ........ | 2,250,000 | 3,050,000 |
| " " " " mining ......... | 1,500,000 | 1,940,000 |
| " " " " manufacturing .. | 3,250,000 | 2,180,000 |

## 45

You join a summer colony within easy rail communication of the city. A general organization of members of the colony controls a central club-house with grounds. The restaurant privilege is sold to outsiders. Facilities are offered to members for tennis, golf, billiards, bowling, boating, swimming. For all these privileges, fees are charged and expenses are incurred. All excess income is to be carried to a general-purpose fund. Entertainments are provided at club expense. You are chosen president of the club.

What ledger accounts should be kept, what items should be carried to each, and what statistics should be gathered ?

# PRESENT WORTHS AND AMOUNTS OF SINGLE PAYMENTS AND OF ANNUITIES

[Chapter XII, pages 159–167]

To give the student ample opportunity for practice in the principles affecting valuation through interest, without the time-destroying labor of making all his own calculations, tables of ratios and of annuity values are given on pages 52 and 53. For assurance that he understands the tables, however, he should do his own figuring for a number of typical problems and compare his results with the tables. A few such typical problems follow.

## 46

(*a*) When money is worth 6 % a year payable in semi-annual installments, what will $1,000 amount to in two years if interest is collected on it, added to the principal, and reinvested ?

(*b*) What is the present worth of $10,000 payable in three years when money is worth 5 % annually ?

(*c*) If you receive the rent of a building at $10,000 a year paid annually at the end of the year, how much will you have at the end of four years, before the fourth payment of rent, if you invest the money as soon as received at 4½ % annually ?

(*d*) When money is worth 5 % a year in semi-annual installments, what is the value today of a series of payments of $1,000 each made at the end of every six months and continued for two years ?

### Table of Ratios

| 2% | 2¼% | 2½% | 3% |
|---|---|---|---|
| .88797138 | .87502427 | .86229687 | .83748426 |
| .90573081 | .89471232 | .88385429 | .86260878 |
| .92384543 | .91484335 | .90595064 | .88848705 |
| .94232233 | .93542732 | .92859941 | .91514166 |
| .96116878 | .95647444 | .95181440 | .94259591 |
| .98039216 | .97799511 | .97560976 | .97087379 |
| 1.00000000 | 1.00000000 | 1.00000000 | 1.00000000 |
| 1.02 | 1.0225 | 1.025 | 1.03 |
| 1.0404 | 1.04550625 | 1.050625 | 1.0609 |
| 1.061208 | 1.06903014 | 1.07689063 | 1.092727 |
| 1.08243216 | 1.09308332 | 1.10381289 | 1.12550881 |
| 1.10408080 | 1.11767769 | 1.13140821 | 1.15927407 |
| 1.12616242 | 1.14282544 | 1.15969342 | 1.19405230 |

| 4% | 4½% | 5% | 6% |
|---|---|---|---|
| .79031453 | .76789574 | .74621540 | .70496054 |
| .82192711 | .80245105 | .78352617 | .74725817 |
| .85480419 | .83856134 | .82270247 | .79209366 |
| .88899636 | .87629660 | .86383760 | .83961928 |
| .92455621 | .91572995 | .90702948 | .88999644 |
| .96153846 | .95693780 | .95238095 | .94339623 |
| 1.00000000 | 1.00000000 | 1.00000000 | 1.00000000 |
| 1.04 | 1.045 | 1.05 | 1.06 |
| 1.0816 | 1.092025 | 1.1025 | 1.1236 |
| 1.124864 | 1.14116613 | 1.157625 | 1.191016 |
| 1.16985856 | 1.19251860 | 1.21550625 | 1.26247696 |
| 1.21665290 | 1.24618194 | 1.27628156 | 1.33822558 |
| 1.26531902 | 1.30226012 | 1.34009564 | 1.41851911 |

## Table of Annuities of $1, Payable at the End of Each Period

*Present Worths*

| | 2% | $2\frac{1}{4}$% | $2\frac{1}{2}$% | 3% |
|---|---|---|---|---|
| 1 | 0.98039216 | 0.97799511 | 0.97560976 | 0.97087379 |
| 2 | 1.94156094 | 1.93446955 | 1.92742415 | 1.91346970 |
| 3 | 2.88388327 | 2.86989687 | 2.85602356 | 2.82861135 |
| 4 | 3.80772870 | 3.78474021 | 3.76197421 | 3.71709840 |
| 5 | 4.71345951 | 4.67945253 | 4.64582850 | 4.57970719 |
| 6 | 5.60143089 | 5.55447680 | 5.50812536 | 5.41719144 |

*Amounts*

| | 2% | $2\frac{1}{4}$% | $2\frac{1}{2}$% | 3% |
|---|---|---|---|---|
| 1 | 1.00 | 1.00 | 1.00 | 1.00 |
| 2 | 2.02 | 2.0225 | 2.025 | 2.03 |
| 3 | 3.0604 | 3.06800625 | 3.075625 | 3.0909 |
| 4 | 4.121608 | 4.13703639 | 4.15251563 | 4.183627 |
| 5 | 5.20404016 | 5.23011971 | 5.25632852 | 5.30913581 |
| 6 | 6.30812096 | 6.34779740 | 6.38773673 | 6.46840988 |

*Present Worths*

| | 4% | $4\frac{1}{2}$% | 5% | 6% |
|---|---|---|---|---|
| 1 | 0.96153846 | 0.95693780 | 0.95238095 | 0.94339623 |
| 2 | 1.88609467 | 1.87266775 | 1.85941043 | 1.83339267 |
| 3 | 2.77509103 | 2.74896435 | 2.72324803 | 2.67301195 |
| 4 | 3.62989522 | 3.58752570 | 3.54595050 | 3.46510561 |
| 5 | 4.45182233 | 4.38997674 | 4.32947667 | 4.21236379 |
| 6 | 5.24213686 | 5.15787248 | 5.07569206 | 4.91732433 |

*Amounts*

| | 4% | $4\frac{1}{2}$% | 5% | 6% |
|---|---|---|---|---|
| 1 | 1.00 | 1.00 | 1.00 | 1.00 |
| 2 | 2.04 | 2.045 | 2.05 | 2.06 |
| 3 | 3.1216 | 3.137025 | 3.1525 | 3.1836 |
| 4 | 4.246464 | 4.27819113 | 4.310125 | 4.374616 |
| 5 | 5.41632256 | 5.47070973 | 5.52563125 | 5.63709296 |
| 6 | 6.63297546 | 6.71689166 | 6.80191281 | 6.97531854 |

## 47

How, from the tables, should you prove or disprove the following statements?

(*a*) The present worth of a payment of $2,000, due in four years, discounted at 3 %, is $1,776.97.

(*b*) If a sinking fund is established and $905.95 is put into it Jan. 1, 1912, and semi-annually for four more payments, and it earns $2\frac{1}{2}$ % a half year, the amount of the fund when the last interest is added, Jan. 1, 1914, will be $4,761.97.

(*c*) If you are entitled for two years to the income of an estate of $100,000 which earns 6 % a year (in half-yearly installments), the present worth, at 6 %, of your title is $11,151.30.

(*d*) You wish to accumulate $10,512.66 in five payments. The sum which you will have to set aside now, and semi-annually thereafter, to attain that sum if the installments earn $2\frac{1}{2}$ % each half year is $2,000.

## 48

Prove, by some other method than that first used, the correctness of your answers to the following:

(*a*) What is the present worth of a payment of $15,500 due in five years, at $4\frac{1}{2}$ % ?

(*b*) You have agreed to pay $9,702.60 three years from today. How much will you have to set aside at intervals of six months, beginning six months from now, to accumulate that sum if the installments earn 3 % semi-annually ?

(*c*) Suppose you wish to buy an annuity of $50,000 a year for two years (in half-yearly installments) to begin six months from now. How much will you have to pay for it now, if interest is at $4\frac{1}{2}$ % ?

(*d*) If a sinking fund of $10,000 is established Jan. 1, 1913, and $10,000 is put into it every six months until July 1, 1915, inclusive, what will be its amount on the latter date, supposing interest to be 3 % semi-annually ?

## FINDING THE VALUE OF A BOND

[Chapter XII, pages 167–169]

### 49

(*a*) What is the present value of the *principal* of a $1,000 bond payable in six years when money is worth 6 % ?

(*b*) What is the present value of the interest payments of a $1,000 bond, bearing 5 % interest, maturing in six years, when money is worth 6 % ?

(*c*) If a business is of such a type that 6 % interest is deemed fair for loans to it, what is the present value of one of its $1,000 bonds payable in six years and bearing 5 % interest ?

(*d*) If a bond pays $50 interest a year and you deem $60 to be a fair payment, what is the present worth, at 6 %, of the first year's loss of interest to you by having this bond rather than another that pays $60 ?

(*e*) What is the present worth of six years' loss of such interest ?

(*f*) What is the premium or discount, on a 6 % basis, on such a bond ?

(*g*) What is the relation between the first three parts of this problem and the last two ?

[If (*g*) is properly answered, the work will be self-proving.]

### 50

Two clerks in an office, A and B, were asked to find the value on a 4 % basis of a $10,000 bond, due in 3 years, bearing interest at 4½ % (semi-annual payments). A reported $10,138.75 and B reported $9,859.96. Show that one or neither was right.

[Will the bond be at a premium or at a discount ? What will be the " difference of interest " ? Will the " difference of interest " be annual or semi-annual ? Will the rate for valuing the annuity be 4½ %, 4 %, 2¼ %, or 2 % ?]

## 51

(*a*) Find directly, without finding the value of the bond, the premium on a bond for $1,000 payable in two years, with interest at 5% (interest semi-annually), when $4\frac{1}{2}$% is the basis rate.

(*b*) How much greater would be the premium on a similar bond paying $5\frac{1}{2}$%?

(*c*) What would be the discount on a bond paying 4%?

(*d*) What would be the discount on a similar bond paying $4\frac{1}{2}$% if the basis were 5%?

(*e*) Should the answer to (*d*) be the same amount as the answer to (*a*)?

[The answers to all but (*e*), but not in the order of the questions, follow: $9.46, $9.40, $9.46, $9.46.]

## 52

Which is a better purchase:

(*a*) A $1,000 5% bond, payable in three years, which you can buy at $101\frac{3}{8}$, if you deem $4\frac{1}{2}$% to be a fair basis, or

(*b*) A $1,000 $4\frac{1}{2}$% bond, payable in three years, which you can buy at $101\frac{1}{2}$, if you deem 4% for this bond a fair basis?

[One is a better bargain than the other by $1.11.]

## AMORTIZATION AND ACCUMULATION

[Chapter XII, pages 169–180]

### 53

Show the amortization table for a 5% bond (interest payable semi-annually), for $1,000, payable in three years, on a basis of 4½% (interest semi-annually).

[The first amortization is $2.19.]

### 54

(*a*) Bonds for $10,000, due January 1, 1917, bearing interest at 6% a year (payable in semi-annual installments), are worth on January 1, 1915, $10,188.10, on the assumption that on security of this class an investment should yield 2½% each half year. Show, by an amortization table, the value of this bond for the first of each January and of each July until maturity.

(*b*) What is the present worth of $100 payable in three periods, when money is worth 2½% per period?

(*c*) What is the relation between the answer to (*b*) and the second amortization of the table in (*a*)?

[The work should be self-proving.]

### 55

Fill in the missing items in the following table:

| Market Interest | Bond Interest | Accumulation | Book Value | Par Value |
|---|---|---|---|---|
| | | | $98,558.06 | $100,000 |
| $1,971.16 | $1,500.00 | | | |
| 1,980.58 | 1,500.00 | | | |
| 1,990.20 | 1,500.00 | | | |

What rate of interest does the bond bear, and what is the basis rate? Can you be sure of these, or are they only one set of answers out of several sets of answers? Could the bond rate be 3%; 6%? After determining the basis rate, fill out the accumulation column directly, by independent calculation, without using any figure in the interest columns.

[This should be self-proving.]

## 56

You are offered two lots of bonds each of $10,000. You would be willing to buy either lot at a price which would yield you a net income of $5\frac{1}{2}$%. Lot A consists of 5% bonds, and lot B consists of 6% bonds. Both pay interest semi-annually, and today is an interest day. Bonds having the term of lot A are listed in bond tables, on a $5\frac{1}{2}$% basis, as having a value six months ago of $9,493.77, and bonds having the term of lot B are listed similarly with a value six months ago of $10,216.00. You are offered lot A at 95, and lot B at 102. Which is the better offer, supposing that in buying the bonds you do not buy the interest coupons due today?

[The offer of one is $7.91 better than the offer of the other.]

## LIFE-MAN'S AND REMAINDER-MAN'S SHARES

[Chapter XII, pages 185–190]

### 57

All of an estate is now in the form of bonds, which bear 5% annual interest ($5,000) and have a present book value of $105,-242.14. You are trustee for the estate. The income of the estate is to go to A.B. for his life, and at his death the principal is to go to C.D. Both are collateral heirs.

(*a*) How much should you pay A.B. at each of the first three interest dates if the bonds were bought on a 4% basis (and continue to be quoted at a price that yields virtually that rate), but reinvestments of small sums can now be made, on equally good security, to yield $4\frac{1}{2}$%?

(*b*) Suppose that the life-man were to die at the end of the third interest period, and that the property of the estate were to be converted into cash at its book value on that date. What would the remainder-man get as his inheritance?

[(*a*): $4,209.69; $4,213.63; $4,217.75. (*b*): $105,242.14.]

## LEASES, PATENTS, AND OTHER ANNUITIES

[Chapter XII, pages 191–194]

### 58

You hold a patent deemed by both you and a friend to be capable of producing an income of $2,000 a year for four years, and after that probably to be worthless. Your friend has a claim to an estate, deemed by both of you to be realizable in three years, for $8,000 (one lump sum). You agree to exchange rights on a 4% basis. How much bonus should be given by one side or the other? What entry will you make on your books at the time of the exchange, supposing the patent right to have been already on your books at the agreed valuation? What entry will you make on your books one year later?

[The difference in value is $147.82.]

### 59

Suppose that six years ago you hired a building on a busy city corner, and got a twelve-year lease, with a stated rental of $10,000 a year. Land values have risen in that vicinity so that the building is now worth $20,000 a year. Supposing that five per cent is considered a fair basis for computation (after allowing for the frequency of rent payments), what is the lease worth today?

If the lease is sold at that value, what entry should be made on the books of the seller of the lease at the time of sale?

What entry should be made on the books of the buyer of the lease at the time of buying? What entry a year later? What entry two years later?

[Value of the lease, $50,756.92. Amounts of certain entries for buyer one year later, $7,462.15 and $2,537.85. Amounts of certain entries two years later, $7,835.26 and $2,164.74.]

## PURCHASE AND SALE OF BONDS

[Chapter XII, pages 179–180, 195–198]

### 60

The following amortization table is correct for a certain bond.

(*a*) What can you tell about the contract terms of the bond ?

(*b*) If you had bought it on December 1, 1912, for $101\frac{3}{4}$ flat, should you have bought it at more or less than its theoretical value, and how much ? What would your entries be ?

(*c*) What entry should you make for the interest received on the bond, November 1, 1913 ?

| Date | Bond Int. | Basis Int. | Amortization | Book Value |
|---|---|---|---|---|
| 1912 May 1 | | | | $10,190.39 |
| Nov. 1 | $250 | $203.81 | $46.19 | 10,144.20 |
| 1913 May 1 | 250 | 202.88 | 47.12 | 10,097.08 |
| Nov. 1 | 250 | 201.94 | 48.06 | 10,049.02 |
| 1914 May 1 | 250 | 200.98 | 49.02 | 10,000.00 |

[Difference, $3.01. Among other things, December 1912, Interest Accrued, $41.67. Among other things, November 1913, Interest Earned, $201.94.]

### 61

Show the ledger accounts (all items) for Bonds, for Interest Earned, and for any gain or loss, after the following transactions:

A 4 % $10,000 bond, paying interest annually on July 1, was bought on July 1 after the interest coupons for that day had been removed, for $87\frac{3}{8}$, which chanced to be its theoretical price on a 4.7 % basis on that day. The bond was sold nine months later for $88\frac{1}{2}$ and interest.

[The gain is $104.50.]

## 62

On January 1 you buy of a friend a bond for $10,449.13, — which is its theoretical value on a 4 % basis. On March 1 you buy another like it, and pay $10,518.79, which includes accrued interest. On July 1, you receive your semi-annual interest of $250 on each bond.

What entry should you make on your books for the original purchase ?

What for the March 1 purchase ?

What for the July 1 interest ?

On October 1 you sell the two bonds on the market for 104 and interest.

How much do you make or lose on the sale ?

What should be the entries for October 1 ?

[Prove your entries by showing that your cash balance equals the gain plus the balance of Interest Earned. The gain is $25.62.]

## 63

A $2,500 bond bearing interest at $4\frac{1}{2}$ % (semi-annual payments) has two years more to run on the day you purchase it. You believe such a bond should pay 3 % semi-annually, and you buy it with that basis in mind, but you pay $2,425 for it. Do you buy at better or worse than that basis ? If you wish to enter the bond on your books at a 6 % basis, what entry will you make for the purchase ? If you sell it three months later at $97\frac{1}{2}$ and interest, what entry will you make for the sale ?

[The balance of Bond Price Residues for both entries will be $4.18. The entry to Interest Earned will be $36.45.]

## ISSUE OF BONDS

[Chapter XII, pages 198–200]

### 64

Bonds are issued to the amount of $12,000,000, payable in twenty-five years, with interest at 5 % annually (in semi-annual payments). The credit of the issuing company is not good enough to warrant investors in lending on a basis of less than $5\frac{1}{2}$ %. The bonds are accordingly sold for $11,190,084.

Show the entry for the issue.

Show the entry for the interest item of six months later, and of twelve months later.

[After the first interest payment, Discount on Bonds has a debit balance of $802,188.69; and after the second interest payment, of $794,248.88.]

### 65

Bonds are issued amounting to $5,000,000, paying 6 % a year (interest semi-annually), and are sold on a 5 % basis. The price is 112.5514.

What entry should be made at issue ?

What should be the entry for the first interest item ? What for the second interest item ?

[At the first interest entry the charge to Bond Premium will be $9,310.75; at the second, $9,543.52.]

## OPTIONAL–REDEMPTION BONDS

[Chapter XII, pages 200–202]

### 66

We find a 5% bond (with interest payable semi-annually), running eighteen years, to have a theoretical value three years from today of $1,054.11 on a 4½% basis. The bond has a clause providing for optional redemption on that date at 104½. Assuming no future change in the market rate of interest or in the security of the bond, what is the bond worth today?

What would the bond be worth today if the optional-redemption figure for three years hence were 106?

[The premium in the first case is $53.26; in the second, $54.11.]

## THE PRINCIPLES OF CAPITALIZATION

[Chapter XIII]

### 67

The following is the abbreviated balance sheet of a corporation, January 1, 1915:

| | | | |
|---|---|---|---|
| Real Estate ........ | $200,000 | Capital Stock ...... | $300,000 |
| Plant ............. | 100,000 | Accounts Payable .. | 25,000 |
| Stock ............. | 50,000 | Surplus ............ | 75,000 |
| Accounts Receivable | 30,000 | | |
| Replacement Fund | 3,500 | | |
| Cash .............. | 16,500 | | |
| | $400,000 | | $400,000 |

The company immediately carries out four operations as follows:

(*a*) It builds a new wharf, in a new location, because engineering difficulties are in the way of extending an old wharf to accommodate larger steamers required for its increased business. The present book value (depreciated in 10 years from $2,000) of the old wharf abandoned is $500, but no recoverable value remains at abandonment, and the cost of the new wharf is $5,000.

(*b*) It buys, out of the replacement fund set aside for the purpose, a new machine at a cost of $3,000, to take the place of one originally costing $4,000 (but now selling new for $3,000) and already written down by depreciation to $500 and yielding $30 as scrap in part payment for the new machine.

(*c*) It buys new machines to replace old (now carried on the books at $2,000) for $10,000, and gives the old for $300 in part payment for the new. The new do the same work as the old but can be operated with less labor (a saving of $1,000 a year) than machines like the old, which originally cost $8,000 and can now be bought for that amount.

(*d*) It discards its old safety devices, which cost $5,000 but have been depreciated to $2,000 (now unsaleable but given in exchange at $50), and in compliance with a new law puts in new safety devices at a cost of $8,000.

Show the balance sheet after the changes above, on these suppositions: no other transactions occur while these operations are going on, and the charges for the purchases described above, not otherwise provided for, were covered by the issue of notes. Show the entry, for each operation, for each of the three bases of capitalization discussed in the chapter.

Supposing the replacement fund had been accumulated specifically for replacing the machines of the second transaction, and that it proves excessive as shown (so that no purpose is served by its continuance), what entry or entries should be made for closing it ?

[It is impossible in a reasonable space to make the description of the circumstances about each of these transactions so detailed that no misconception can arise. The purpose of the problem is to arouse discussion in a class rather than to show an absolutely right or wrong conclusion. Taking each circumstance on its face, however, the three bases of capitalization give the following balance-sheet items: cost basis — Plant, $122,950, Surplus, $72,330; duplication basis — Plant, $121,000, Surplus, $70,380; earning-capacity basis — Plant, $118,000, Surplus, $67,380.

What is the actual gain in the second case from the reduction in the purchase price of the new machine ? Is it a gain of cash ? of capital ? of surplus ? of saved expense ?]

## RAILROAD ACCOUNTS

[Chapter XIV]

### 68

Arrange the following items of a railroad report in the form that will give the best idea of its condition and earning capacity:

[All figures are in millions.]

| | |
|---|---|
| Due to other companies | $1.5 |
| Securities owned and unpledged | 145.0 |
| Interest on bonds owned | 3.9 |
| Dividends declared but not due | 6.4 |
| Cash | 10.3 |
| Advances to other companies | 18.3 |
| Dividends, 4 % on preferred stock | 3.2 |
| Reserve for depreciation of securities | 35.4 |
| Due from agents | .7 |
| Miscellaneous income | .1 |
| Interest on funded debt | 14.0 |
| Other investments | .2 |
| Common stock outstanding | 202.3 |
| Matured obligations | .4 |
| Miscellaneous rental charges | .5 |
| Materials and supplies | 8.3 |
| Dividends due but uncalled for | 4.5 |
| Interest earned on miscellaneous accounts | 4.2 |
| Interest receivable not due | 2.2 |
| Surplus for the year | 11.7 |
| Dividends, 9 % on common stock | 18.2 |
| Road and equipment | 525.9 |
| Reserve for special funds | .4 |
| Rental charges for joint facilities | 1.0 |
| Dividends receivable not due | .3 |
| Special deposits | .1 |
| Hire of equipment — debit balance | .8 |
| Allowance for depreciation on road and equipment | 15.1 |
| Net income | 33.1 |

| | |
|---|---|
| Preferred stock outstanding | $79.5 |
| Due from other companies | 2.0 |
| Dividends on stock owned | 8.3 |
| Securities pledged | 68.7 |
| Rail operations — revenue | 88.3 |
| Reserve for extra dividend | 54.0 |
| Prepayments of various expenses | 1.4 |
| Gain on sales of stock | 16.2 |
| Outside operations — expenses | 3.0 |
| Rents receivable not due | .1 |
| Allowance for insurance | .6 |
| Miscellaneous rentals earned | .4 |
| Loans and bills receivable | 18.4 |
| Matured interest payable | 4.0 |
| Profit and Loss | 90.5 |
| Rentals earned from lease of road | .1 |
| Miscellaneous accounts receivable | 5.0 |
| Contracts for land sales (liability) | 1.2 |
| Mortgage bonds outstanding | 241.9 |
| Rentals earned from joint facilities | .8 |
| Miscellaneous deferred liabilities | 2.1 |
| Contracts for land sales (asset) | 1.2 |
| Cash and securities in special funds | .4 |
| Audited vouchers payable | 5.7 |
| Railway operating income | 31.6 |
| Premium on stock issued | 20.0 |
| Taxes accrued not due | 2.5 |
| Assets set aside ready for paym't of a spec'l divid. | 54.0 |
| Miscellaneous bonds outstanding | 72.1 |
| Rail operations — expenses | 51.4 |
| Accounts payable | 4.7 |
| Taxes | 5.1 |
| Interest payable not due | 1.5 |
| Outside operations — revenue | 2.8 |

[The items are grouped naturally as follows, in millions: $724.7, $44.7, $2.6, $21.4, $54.0, total assets, $847.4; $301.8, $314.0, $20.8, $10.4, $20.1,[1] $89.8, $90.5, total liabilities $847.4; $36.9,

[1] This road reports the gain on stocks sold as a deferred liability, for the gain has not yet been appropriated to any ultimate destination.

– $.2, $36.7, $5.1, $31.6, $17.8, $49.4, $16.3, $33.1, $21.4, surplus for the year $11.7.]

## 69

Following are the abbreviated balance-sheet figures (for the end of each year) and income-sheet figures of a railroad for three years [all figures in millions]:

*Assets*

| | First year | Second year | Third year |
|---|---|---|---|
| Cost of road and equipment | $152.5 | $160.4 | $166.7 |
| Real estate, etc. | 1.0 | 1.1 | 1.0 |
| Improvements and betterments | 2.4 | 3.4 | 3.5 |
| Investments | 31.4 | 30.2 | 29.7 |
| Advances to subsidiaries | 3.3 | 3.6 | 4.7 |
| Supplies | 3.8 | 5.5 | 6.5 |
| Cash | 1.1 | 8.8 | 8.8 |
| Other current assets | 3.4 | 4.3 | 5.7 |
| Bonds and notes guaranteed | 3.7 | 3.3 | 3.4 |
| | $202.6 | $220.6 | $230.0 |

*Liabilities*

| | First year | Second year | Third year |
|---|---|---|---|
| Capital stock | $60.0 | $60.0 | $60.0 |
| Bonded debt | 114.4 | 129.2 | 128.5 |
| Bills payable | | | 6.5 |
| Accounts payable | 2.6 | 2.2 | 2.5 |
| Mileage coupons outstanding | .1 | .1 | .1 |
| Dividends declared | 1.8 | 1.8 | 1.8 |
| Other current liabilities | 4.8 | 5.4 | 6.1 |
| Reserve for depreciation of special tracks | .3 | .5 | .3 |
| Contingent liability on guarantees | 3.7 | 3.3 | 3.4 |
| Profit and loss | 14.9 | 18.1 | 20.8 |
| | $202.6 | $220.6 | $230.0 |

*Income Sheet*

| | First year | Second year | Third year |
|---|---|---|---|
| Gross earnings | $38.5 | $43.0 | $48.3 |
| Operating expenses | 26.5 | 30.9 | 35.8 |
| Net earnings | 12.0 | 12.1 | 12.5 |
| Rents earned | .9 | .7 | .7 |
| Income from investments | .7 | .8 | .8 |
| Gross income | 13.6 | 13.6 | 14.0 |
| Fixed charges | 6.8 | 7.3 | 7.6 |
| Net income | 6.8 | 6.3 | 6.4 |
| Dividends | 3.6 | 3.6 | 3.6 |
| Surplus for the year | $3.2 | $2.7 | $2.8 |

Following are significant statistical and expense figures:

| | First year | Second year | Third year |
|---|---|---|---|
| Pass. train earnings per revenue train mile | $1.314 | $1.231 | $1.284 |
| Frt. train earnings per revenue train mile | $1.813 | $1.853 | $1.851 |
| Average paid each passenger per mile | 2.289c. | 2.434c. | 2.368c. |
| Average paid each ton per mile | .791c. | .803c. | .801c. |
| Passengers per train mile | 46.8 | 41.1 | 44.8 |
| Tons per train mile | 229 | 230.6 | 230.9 |
| Pass. train expenses per revenue train mile | $.796 | $.869 | $.904 |
| Frt. train expenses per revenue train mile | $1.32 | $1.37 | $1.42 |
| Average length of passenger journey, miles | 39 | 34 | 40 |
| Average haul of freight, miles | 167 | 160 | 168 |
| Net revenue per passenger train mile | $.518 | $.362 | $.380 |
| Net revenue per freight train mile | $.493 | $.483 | $.431 |
| Average number loaded cars per frt. train | 13.3 | 12.9 | 12.4 |
| Average number empty cars per frt. train | 6.5 | 5.8 | 5.5 |
| Passengers carried | 9,500,000 | 10,600,000 | 10,900,000 |
| Ton miles carried [billions] | 3.5 | 3.9 | 4.4 |
| Fuel cost | $2,200,000 | $2,560,000 | $2,910,000 |
| Train wages | $2,000,000 | $2,660,000 | $3,350,000 |
| Maintenance of way, per mile | $1,500 | $1,600 | $1,860 |
| Maintenance of locomotives, per mile | 6.7c. | 9.1c. | 7.7c. |
| Maintenance of passenger cars, per mile | 1.3c. | 1.6c. | 1.5c. |
| Maintenance of freight cars, per mile | .82c. | .86c. | 1.05c. |
| Par value of stocks held | $25,800,000 | | |
| Book value of stocks held | 17,400,000 | | |
| Par value of bonds held | 14,100,000 | | |
| Book value of bonds held | 14,000,000 | | |

Explain: the reason for the increase of bonded debt in the second year; the source of the funds for additions to cost of road in the third year; the grounds for accepting or rejecting the valuation of stocks and bonds owned; the probability that the surplus is real; the reason for the decline in net income; the proper place for the bills payable — capital or current liabilities; the decline in gross earnings per passenger-train mile; the increase in average freight-train load; the decline in net earnings per freight-train mile; the increase in expenses, passenger and freight, per mile.

## REORGANIZATIONS

### [Chapter XV]

### 70

A railroad's capital liabilities are as follows:

| | |
|---|---|
| $25,000,000 | common stock |
| 25,000,000 | preferred stock (6 %) |
| 5,000,000 | income bonds (5 %) |
| 15,000,000 | general first-mortgage bonds ($4\frac{1}{2}$ %) |
| 5,000,000 | general second-mortgage bonds ($4\frac{1}{2}$ %) |
| 10,000,000 | car-trust bonds (5 %) |

The net earnings of the road have run for the last five years as follows, — $950,000, $1,150,000, $1,350,000, $1,050,000, $1,150,000; its other income has been steady at $500,000; its fixed charges in addition to interest have been close to $100,000. Rentals and taxes have now increased $250,000; earnings have shrunk slightly owing to hard times; and so the fixed charges cannot be met.

Assuming a reorganization to be necessary, and no unusual privileges to attach to any of the liabilities specified above, outline a plan for reorganization for each of the following circumstances:

(*a*) The stockholders believe the road can be developed under new management, with new capital, to yield in the near future 5 % on the preferred stock and in the remote future 5 % on the common stock.

(*b*) No one believes the road can ever yield any dividends on common stock, but everyone believes it may in ten years yield 4 or 5 % on preferred stock.

(*c*) The road does not need new capital, but must wait several years for the country to develop to its requirements for traffic — perhaps two years for earnings enough to pay its present fixed charges, four years for enough to pay interest on income bonds, six years for dividends on preferred stock, and eight years for dividends on common stock.

(*d*) The bondholders have no confidence in the management of the road, but have large confidence in its present earning capacity if well managed; and the stockholders have much confidence in the management but little confidence in the earning capacity.

# TRUST ACCOUNTING

[Chapter XVII]

## 71

When a trust is taken over on July 1, the property in it is as follows (using appraised value for all items except cash): bonds, $39,700; real estate, $159,000; cash, $1,300. The compensation for handling the property is 4½ %.

On January 1, interest is collected on bonds, $700; rentals are collected on real estate, $3,850; amortization for the half year on the bonds is $40; repairs on real estate are paid for, $210.

On March 1, rent is collected, $4,000, and $1,000 is paid to the owner of the income.

On July 1, interest is collected, $700, and $41 is set aside for amortization; and taxes are paid, $3,800. The balance of income is transferred to principal. Half the bonds are sold for $20,000.

Show the balance sheet for the trust company for these transactions at this stage.

[The total of the balance sheet is $204,349.50.]

# INSURANCE AND LIFE TENURES

[Chapter XVIII]

## 72

An employee of yours desires a technical education, and your confidence in him justifies a belief that he will be worth to you $2,000 a year after a four-year course in a technical school. He agrees to work for you for three years after his four-year course is completed, for $500 a year, if you will advance to him $850 a year (the first payment to be immediate) for four years to enable him to take such a course. Counting the risk of his death before the contract is completed, is the offer approximately fair ?

To avoid detailed calculation of great refinement, assume that you count the risk as $3,400 (the maximum outstanding advance at any time) for seven years, and that the benefit of your employee's services after his return to work will not be realized until the end of any year — though in reality your risk is only $850 for one year, $1,700 for one year, etc., and your gain from his services will begin at the beginning of the fifth year. Assume the man's age to be 25, and that you will not take out a policy on his life but will take the risk yourself. Assume money to be worth 5 % for the loan, but to be calculated at only 4 % in determining the cost of insurance. Suppose the cost of paid-up insurance has already been calculated for five years, for men 25 years of age, as follows: present worth of $1,000 death claims, on the standard number of lives (89,032), maturing in ages 25 to 29 inclusive, $3,197,200; or cost of $1,000 paid-up insurance, without loading, for those years $35.91. Suppose, further, that the number of deaths on the standard number of lives for age 30 is 719, and for the next year is the same.

[The present worth of what you are to do for your employee is $3,164.76, and the cost of insurance is $164.66, or a total of $3,329.42. The present worth of what he is to do for you is $3,360.63. The offer is therefore to your advantage, especially as the calculation has somewhat overstated the risk to be insured and somewhat understated the value of his services. (To enable the student to perform all the calculations for himself, without using the cost of paid-up insurance for five years as given in the problem, the following table is appended.)

| Age | Living | Dying |
|---|---|---|
| 25 | 89,032 | 718 |
| 26 | 88,314 | 718 |
| 27 | 87,596 | 718 |
| 28 | 86,878 | 718 |
| 29 | 86,160 | 719 |
| 30 | 85,441 | 719 |
| 31 | 84,722 | 719] |

## 73

A piece of real estate is sold at auction subject to the widow's right of dower, for $10,000. Her right of dower is the right to one-third of the income of the property for her life. Assume her expectation of life to be five years, and interest to be 5 % annually.

If the auction price was fair, what is the property worth ? What is a fair cash offer to make to the widow in exchange for her surrender of the right of dower ?

[Value of the property, $10,777.70. Value of right of dower, $777.70.]

## FACTORY ACCOUNTING

[Chapter XIX]

### 74

The following facts refer to an establishment as a whole:

| | |
|---|---|
| Working year, 2,700 hours | |
| Ground rent, annually | $2,000 |
| Light, annually | 350 |
| Heat, annually | 500 |
| Depreciation of buildings, 3 % | |
| Depreciation of machinery, 10 % | |
| Insurance, 1 % | |
| Taxes, $1\frac{1}{2}$ % | |
| Interest, 5 % | |

The following refer to the power plant:

| | |
|---|---|
| Valuation of building | 3,000 |
| Valuation of machinery | 10,000 |
| Annual repairs of building | 30 |
| Annual repairs of machinery | 300 |
| Wages annually | 1,500 |
| Supplies consumed annually | 75 |
| Fuel consumed annually | 1,500 |
| Share of land occupied, 1/5 | |
| Share of light consumed, 1/7 | |
| Run full capacity all the time | |

The following refer to the shop:

| | |
|---|---|
| Valuation of building | 15,000 |
| Valuation of machinery | 75,000 |
| Annual repairs of building | 300 |
| Janitor care, etc. | 1,350 |
| Annual repairs of machinery | 2,000 |
| Oil, waste, etc., consumed annually | 243 |
| Share of heat consumed, 4/5 | |
| Share of light consumed, 5/7 | |
| Share of power consumed, 9/10 | |
| Share of land occupied, 2/5 | |

The following refer to machine #57:

Annual charge for use of special tools ............ 6.20

Share of all general shop charges, based on its proportion of valuation, of space, of power, etc., assuming all these to give the same proportion, 1/45

No idle time, and setting-up time negligible.

Find the machine hour-rate for machine #57, and by such a calculation that the minimum number of changes will be required for another machine, with different proportions, in the same shop.

[Answer, $.2111.]

## 75

Find the minimum rate and the additional rate for another machine (#83) in the shop for which figures were given in Problem 74, when the following figures can be attached to the machine itself:

| | |
|---|---|
| Cost of machine | $950.00 |
| Supplies consumed annually | 2.50 |
| Superintendence | 75.00 |
| Annual charge for use of special tools | 2.30 |
| Care | 4.80 |
| Repairs from operation | 16.00 |
| Obsolescence | 28.00 |
| Depreciation from operation | 21.50 |
| Power, 1/50 of total of plant | |
| Space, 1/75 of total of shop | |
| Heat, 1/40 of total of shop | |
| Light, 1/50 of total of shop | |

The specific items given above for this machine supplant, of course, the corresponding blanket figures of the previous problem: e. g., here is given a specific cost for supplies used with this machine, and separate shares for heat, light, etc.; therefore these figures supplant the $243 for supplies, and the 1/45 for general shop costs, of the other problem.

[The minimum hour rate is $.0640, and the additional rate is $.0873.]

## 76

The following facts apply to machine #19 for the year:

| | | | |
|---|---|---|---|
| Space cost | $29.25 | Use cost | $85.66 |
| Machine cost | 69.00 | Power cost | 47.25 |
| Estimated idleness | | | one-half |

Assuming a nine-hour day and a year of 2,700 hours, show the machine ledger for machine #19 for one day when the occupied time is 8 hours, and the running time 6 hours.

Order #25 was the only job on the machine that day, and it was begun and finished on that day. Show the charge to the order for its machine-burden items.

[Answer, 88c.]

## 77

Order #99 was on machine #10, in Dept. A, 9 hours, of which the machine was running 8 hours. The records show that the machine is idle, on the average, five-sixteenths of the time.

The total group costs of machine #10 for the year are as follows:

| | | | |
|---|---|---|---|
| Space cost | $27.30 | Use cost | $89.41 |
| Machine cost | 103.00 | Power cost | 94.50 |

The cost figures for the shop are as follows:

| | |
|---|---|
| Raw material used | $180,000 |
| Secondary stores cost | 3,000 |
| Superintendence Dept. A | 4,000 |
| " " B | 2,000 |
| " " C | 3,500 |
| Total direct labor charges Dept. A | 60,000 |
| " " " " " B | 45,000 |
| " " " " " C | 50,000 |
| Total manufacturing cost exclusive of administration, Dept. A | 900,000 |
| Total manufacturing cost exclusive of administration, Dept. B | 110,000 |
| Total manufacturing cost exclusive of administration, Dept. C | 120,000 |

| | |
|---|---|
| Administrative expense, Dept. A | 3,000 |
| " " " B | 5,000 |
| " " " C | 7,000 |
| General factory administrative expense | 25,000 |
| Selling cost | 40,000 |

The following costs have been already charged to order # 99:

| | | | |
|---|---|---|---|
| Labor | $25.00 | Stores | $12.60 |

Show all charges to order # 99 assuming that in this business a percentage basis is satisfactory for all distributions for which no other basis is implied above.

[Answer, $43.11.]

## 78

The following figures are taken from the trial balance and from a supplementary statement of a corporation:

| | | |
|---|---|---|
| Capital Stock | | $100,000 |
| Bills Payable | | 25,900 |
| Accounts Receivable | $74,000 | |
| Accounts Payable | | 31,000 |
| Wages | | 137,000 |
| Pay Roll | 130,000 | |
| Raw Material Inventory | 17,000 | |
| Raw Materials | 48,000 | 50,000 |
| Goods-in-Process Inventory | 33,000 | |
| Manufacturing | 187,000 | |
| Rent | 4,000 | |
| Interest | 300 | |
| Insurance | 600 | |
| Plant | 50,000 | |
| Taxes | 1,000 | |
| General Expense | 7,000 | |
| Cash | 4,000 | |
| Selling Cost | 8,000 | |
| Sales | | 220,000 |
| | $563,900 | $563,900 |

*Supplementary facts*

| | |
|---|---|
| Goods in process, on hand, at cost ........... | $23,000 |
| Interest accrued liability .................... | 300 |
| Insurance premiums unexpired .............. | 150 |
| Finished goods on hand ...................... | 13,000 |
| Raw material on hand ........................ | 15,000 |

Show the income sheet and the balance sheet.

[They should prove each other. The balance sheet total is $179,150.]

## 79

Suppose that the cost accounts of a manufacturing business are carried through the general ledger, and that the accounts have been closed so far as to show on the ledger all the figures for the operating statement. This statement follows on the next page.

*Operating statement, May 1, 1913 to April 30, 1914*

| | | | |
|---|---|---|---|
| Sales ........................ | | | $297,000 |
| Raw materials on hand, 5/1/13 ... | | $26,000 | |
| " " bought ........... | | 107,000 | |
| " " handled .......... | | 133,000 | |
| " " on hand, 4/30/14 .. | | 18,000 | |
| " " consumed ........ | | 115,000 | |
| Wages paid ............ | $54,000 | | |
| Less balance due, 5/1/13 . | 2,000 | | |
| | 52,000 | | |
| Wages due, 4/30/14 .... | 900 | | |
| Wages cost .................... | | 52,900 | |
| Taxes ........................ | | 1,500 | |
| Interest prepaid, 5/1/13 . | 600 | | |
| Interest paid in and for year | 1,000 | 1,600 | |
| General manufacturing expenses .. | | 30,000 | |
| Manufacturing cost ............ | | 201,000 | |
| Goods in process, 5/1/13 ........ | | 10,000 | |
| Cost of goods for year ........... | | 211,000 | |
| Goods in process, 4/30/14 ....... | | 7,000 | |
| Cost of goods finished in year .... | | 204,000 | |
| Stock on hand, 5/1/13 .......... | | 60,000 | |
| Cost of finished goods handled.... | | 264,000 | |
| Stock on hand, 4/30/14 .......... | | 20,000 | |
| Cost of goods sold .............. | | 244,000 | |
| Selling cost .................... | | 10,000 | 254,000 |
| Net profits .................... | | | $43,000 |

Show the debit and credit ledger *totals* (not balances) for these cost accounts.

[The excess of total debits over total credits is $1,100; but the total for each account should prove with the figures of the operating statement above.]

## 80

Show the balance sheet for a business which meets the following conditions: capital stock, $200,000; cash on hand, $7,000; surplus, $50,000; manufactured goods on hand, $10,000; notes outstanding, $25,000; sums owed for raw material, $25,000; sums owed for wages, $3,000; raw material on hand, $6,000; undivided profits, $4,000; notes of customers on hand, $17,000; depreciation fund, in bonds, $8,000; sums due from customers, $15,000; real estate, $100,000; machinery, etc., $144,000.

In the following year the business is as follows: goods manufactured (on contract) and accepted by customers, though some await orders for shipment, $147,000 (contract price); goods delivered (on contract), $135,000, of which the goods on hand at the beginning of the year made up $13,000, and the new product showed a cost of $111,500; collected on goods, $129,000 in cash, $20,000 in notes; labor expense incurred and paid, $50,000; raw material bought, $75,000; raw material paid for, $90,000; raw material consumed, $70,000; new machinery bought and paid for, $20,000; interest paid, $1,000; interest accrued against the corporation, not yet due, $200; cash spent for current maintenance of buildings and machinery, $3,500; collected on notes, $28,000; general expenses paid, $9,000; borrowed on notes, $50,000; restoration of buildings, paid from depreciation fund, $2,000; paid on notes, $20,000; losses from bad debts, $1,000; taxes paid, $1,000; dividends paid, $17,500.

Show the income sheet for the year.

Show the balance sheet for the beginning of the new year.

[Surplus, $47,800.]

[It is probable that time will be saved and confusion will be avoided if a rough journal and a rough ledger are used for assistance in working out this problem.]

## 81

The following figures are shown on a balance sheet for January 1, 1913:

| | | | |
|---|---|---|---|
| Real Estate | $100,000 | Capital Stock | $400,000 |
| Machinery | 500,000 | Funded Debt | 200,000 |
| Merchandise | 150,000 | Bills Payable | 50,000 |
| Accounts Receivable | 50,000 | Accounts Payable | 75,000 |
| Cash | 50,000 | Surplus | 125,000 |
| | $850,000 | | $850,000 |

The following is the income sheet for the year 1912:

| | | |
|---|---|---|
| Sales | $1,000,000 | |
| Goods in process, Dec. 31, 1912 | 30,000 | |
| Stores on hand, Dec. 31, 1912 | 20,000 | |
| Merchandise, Dec. 31, 1912 | 100,000 | |
| | $1,150,000 | |
| Less selling costs | 250,000 | $900,000 |
| Goods in process, Jan. 1, 1912 | $20,000 | |
| Stores on hand, Jan. 1, 1912 | 15,000 | |
| Merchandise on hand, Jan. 1, 1912 | 80,000 | |
| Supplies purchased | 175,000 | |
| Wages paid | 320,000 | |
| Wages due and unpaid | 30,000 | |
| General manufacturing expenses | 200,000 | |
| Cost of product | | $840,000 |
| Net profit | | 60,000 |
| Dividends declared, but not yet paid | | 32,000 |
| Surplus for the year | | $28,000 |

Is the balance sheet consistent with the income sheet? If not, assume the ledger and the totals of both sides of the balance sheet to be correct, and any error to have been caused by unwarranted combinations or cancellations of accounts, and then correct the balance sheet.

Show the ledger, with both sides of all manufacturing accounts, when closed for December 31, 1912.

The balance sheet on January 1, 1912, was as follows:

| | | | |
|---|---|---|---|
| Real Estate ........ | $100,000 | Capital Stock ..... | $400,000 |
| Machinery .......... | 500,000 | Funded Debt ..... | 200,000 |
| Goods in Process .... | 20,000 | Bills Payable ...... | 40,000 |
| Finished Goods ..... | 80,000 | Accounts Payable | 60,000 |
| Stores .............. | 15,000 | Surplus ........... | 97,000 |
| Accounts Receivable | 75,000 | Dividends ........ | 28,000 |
| Cash ............... | 35,000 | | |
| | $825,000 | | $825,000 |

Is this consistent with the income sheet and with the 1913 balance sheet as corrected ?

[The work should be self-proving.]

## 82

Prepare such a tabular statement or statements as an accountant should give to his employers or clients for a business yielding the following figures on three trial balances (of ledger *balances*) taken at the times indicated.

| | Trial balance at the opening of business, Jan. 1, 1912 | | Trial balance Dec. 31, 1912, before the books are closed | | Trial balance at the opening of business, Jan. 1, 1913 | |
|---|---|---|---|---|---|---|
| | Dr. | Cr. | Dr. | Cr. | Dr. | Cr. |
| Capital Stock .......... | .... | $200,000 | .... | $200,000 | .... | $200,000 |
| Bills Payable .......... | .... | 30,000 | .... | 40,000 | .... | 40,000 |
| Accounts Payable ...... | .... | 35,000 | .... | 37,500 | .... | 37,500 |
| Surplus ................ | .... | 7,000 | .... | 7,000 | .... | 9,000 |
| Dividends Declared ..... | .... | 10,000 | .... | .... | .... | 10,000 |
| Real Estate and Plant .. | $135,000 | .... | $137,500 | .... | $137,500 | .... |
| Accounts Receivable .... | 88,200 | .... | 80,200 | .... | 80,200 | .... |
| Goods in Process ....... | 17,000 | .... | 17,000 | .... | 20,000 | .... |
| Finished Goods ......... | 25,000 | .... | 25,000 | .... | 23,000 | .... |
| Raw Materials Inventory | 15,000 | .... | 15,000 | .... | 35,000 | .... |
| Raw Materials ......... | .... | .... | 57,000 | .... | .... | .... |
| Wages ................ | .... | 7,000 | 52,000 | .... | .... | 2,000 |
| Taxes ................ | .... | 200 | 2,300 | .... | .... | 200 |
| Insurance ............. | 1,000 | .... | 2,200 | .... | 1,000 | .... |
| General Expenses ....... | .... | .... | 7,500 | .... | .... | .... |
| Sales .................. | .... | .... | .... | 113,200 | .... | .... |
| Cash ................. | 8,000 | .... | 2,000 | .... | 2,000 | .... |
| | $289,200 | $289,200 | $397,700 | $397,700 | $298,700 | $298,700 |

[The work should be self-proving.]

## MUNICIPAL ACCOUNTING

[Chapter XX]

### 83

A city department on July 1 is authorized to make charges or levies or assessments that will give it an estimated revenue of $3,000,000. On August 1 it sends out bills for $1,500,000. On September 1 it is authorized to make expenditures or incur liabilities for $2,500,000. On October 1 it enters into contracts involving expenditures of $500,000. On November 1 it collects on bills $750,000 in cash. On December 1 it places orders for purchases on the open market for $100,000. On January 1 it pays for its open-market purchases and pays $200,000 on contract liabilities.

(*a*) Show the accounts, and the balance sheet, that will give the officials full information regarding the status of their balances — revenues, appropriations, expected receipts, current cash, liabilities, etc., — without interfering with the ordinary bookkeeping of the treasurer and collector.

(*b*) Suppose the department were authorized to borrow cash, in anticipation of revenues, and to issue obligations therefor, not exceeding $100,000 at par, and had used that authority, on July 15, for a loan of $100,000. What entries should you recommend for presenting information akin to that given by the entries required above? (New accounts, with expressive titles, may be established if necessary.)

[The balance sheet required by (*a*) gives a total of $2,700,000.]

### 84

A city contributes $17,500 at the beginning of each year for five years to a sinking fund. Suppose the cash in the fund, including income, is always invested as soon as available, either in 4 % bonds at par or on the market at 4 %. Make the entries and show the balance sheet at the end of the time after the income has been added to the principal.

[Total of the balance sheet, $98,577.07.]

## THE NATURE OF COMMERCIAL DISCOUNTS

[Chapter XXI, pages 340–342]

### 85

Accepting the theory that merchandise discounts forfeited are more important to watch than discounts taken and given, and that the offering of discounts is in reality only a device for offering merchandise at a normal price to those who do not ask extended credit, show what entry is necessary, in each of the following cases, to record all the desired facts when the bill is paid. Goods are supposed to be both bought and sold on terms of 6% discount when payment is made in 10 days, 5% in 30 days, net in 60 days, and in every case the figure given below is the full amount of the bill.

On January 1, Doe pays his invoice of November 2, amounting to $500; Hoe pays his of December 2, amounting to $1,000; Roe pays his of December 22, amounting to $200.

On the same day, you pay to Poe your bill of December 2, $300, and to Coe your bill of December 22, $700.

[The new debits to Merchandise (or Sales) should be $102; the credits to Merchandise (or Purchases) should be $60; the credits to Collected Discounts, $40; the debits to Neglected Discounts, $3; the debits to Cash, $1,638; the credits to Cash, $943; the debits to Accounts Payable, $1,000; the credits to Accounts Receivable, $1,700.]

## THE NATURE OF PROPRIETORSHIP PROFITS

[Chapter XXI, pages 342–346]

### 86

Below are shown on ledger accounts all the facts of relationship between the proprietor of a business, who gives all his time to it, and the business itself. How far do these accounts help in answering these two questions:

(*a*) Supposing the proprietor is offered a salary of $8,000 as manager of another business, on condition that he give up his own, will he presumably gain or lose (assuming that no change in the profitableness of his own business would occur if he should remain with it) by accepting the offer?

(*b*) If a corporation is to be organized to buy out the business, and it is presumed that the change of legal form will have no appreciable effect on the amount of business done or on the economy or profit with which it is done, how should you go to work to determine what capitalization will presumably allow 8 % dividends?

PROPRIETOR'S CAPITAL ACCOUNT

| | | | | | |
|---|---|---|---|---|---|
| | | | Jan. 1, 1914 | Balance | 125,000 [1] |

PROPRIETOR'S DRAWING ACCOUNT

| | | | | | |
|---|---|---|---|---|---|
| July 15, 1914 | Cash | 5,000 | Dec. 31, 1914 | Profit and Loss | 10,000 [2] |
| Dec. 31, 1914 | Cash | 5,000 | | | |

[1] The assets are conservatively valued, and are readily saleable.

[2] This represents a fair average over a series of years.

## CONSOLIDATIONS

[Chapter XXI, pages 346–351]

### 87

Four businesses yield the following statistics:

| Business | Net Average Assets | Net Average Income |
|---|---|---|
| A | $300,000 | $36,000 |
| B | 50,000 | 10,000 |
| C | 150,000 | 24,000 |
| D | 140,000 | 14,000 |

Consolidation is supposed to increase profits, of the combination, by $28,000 over the combined profits of the individual businesses, and capitalization is to be on a 10% basis. What stock shall be given to each business entering the combination if each is to be given stock at par for its old assets, which chance to be appraised at the figures of the net average assets above, and such stock in addition as is warranted by the suppositions shown below?

(*a*) The difference in earning capacity of the old businesses was due not to difference of management but to difference of opportunity, and hence any difference in income of the consolidation will arise from the changed scale of business and from the unified control.

(*b*) The old differences in income were presumably due to differences in efficiency of management, and hence the gain from consolidation will arise chiefly from the fact that the better management of the businesses previously more profitable will now extend over those previously less profitable; the stock to be issued for the anticipated gain by consolidation is therefore to be distributed on the basis of the evidence of previous good management, and the stock representing old good will is to be distributed on the basis of old good will.

(*c*) To both of the arrangements above someone desired in the combination refuses to agree, and a compromise is made under which all the stock to be issued above the appraised value of the assets is to be distributed on the basis of old good will.

If the managers of D still refuse to enter the combination and their participation is desired, what adjustment can be made in the plan without interfering with its automatic character, and how will it work out?

[(*a*) A, $525,000; B, $87,500; C, $262,500; D, $245,000
(*b*) A, $391,100;[1] B, $255,600;[1] C, $333,300;[1] D, $140,000
(*c*) A, $444,000; B, $170,000; C, $366,000; D, $140,000]

[1] Small balances of less than one share would be adjusted by cash settlements.

## INSOLVENCY SETTLEMENTS

[Chapter XXII, pages 354–362]

### 88

A business is in financial difficulties with the following balance sheet:

| | | | |
|---|---|---|---|
| Accounts Receivable . | $35,000 | Partners . . . . . . . . . . . . | $40,000 |
| Merchandise . . . . . . . . | 44,500 | Accounts Payable . . . | 43,000 |
| Cash . . . . . . . . . . . . . . . | 3,000 | Bills Payable . . . . . . . . | 12,000 |
| Bonds . . . . . . . . . . . . . . | 14,000 | Wages due . . . . . . . . . . | 1,000 |
| | | Taxes due . . . . . . . . . . | 500 |
| | $96,500 | | $96,500 |

Of the accounts receivable, $20,000 are estimated to be good; $7,000, probably worth $3,000; $8,000, worthless. The merchandise is probably worth $12,000. The bonds, presumably worth book value, are pledged as security for the bills payable. The estimated cost of liquidation (fees, expenses, etc.) is $3,000. Show the statement of affairs, with the probable percentage of payment on unsecured balances.

In the process of liquidation, the accounts receivable yield $23,000, the merchandise, $16,000, the bonds, $9,500; the expense of liquidation is $3,000. Show the accounts for the process of liquidation, including the deficiency account.

What is the actual percentage of payment on unsecured balances?

[Estimated percentage of payment on unsecured balances, 82.56; actual percentage of unsecured balances paid, 82.42. Deficiency account debits: Realization, $45,000; Expenses of Liquidation, $3,000. Deficiency account credits: Liquidation, $8,000; Partners, $40,000.]

## 89

A firm's assets are found to be as follows: cash, $2,000; land and buildings (conservatively estimated, but mortgaged for $8,000), $10,000; plant and equipment (conservatively estimated, but mortgaged for $9,000), $20,000; unfinished goods in process of manufacture, probably worth cost, $30,000; bonds owned (of which $6,000 have been put up as collateral for a $5,000 loan included in bills payable), worth the book value of $14,500; materials on hand (probably saleable for $500), $2,000; book accounts (of which one-half are deemed good and the other half worth three-quarters of the book figures), $6,000. The debts are as follows (besides the mortgages mentioned above): trade creditors, $43,400; bills payable, $16,000; taxes and wages accrued, $1,300; liability on endorsements of past-due notes which the firm has discounted, but on which it probably cannot recover, $13,000. The partners' capital has remained unchanged on the books throughout the year at $50,000, but operations have resulted in a loss, shown on the profit and loss account, of $43,200.

Make out a statement of affairs, assuming that the expenses of liquidation will be $1,450.

Suppose that the actual realization falls short of the estimates by $3,000, but the estimate of expenses is correct. Show the accounts for realization and liquidation, including the deficiency account.

[The deficiency account will show debits and credits of $62,900 each.]

# APPENDIX A

## SPECIAL FORMS AND BOOKS

[Pages 369–396]

### 90

Arrange a form of cash book (receipts and disbursements) for the entry both of payments by customers and of payments by the business of bills (less any discounts for early payment) already entered to Accounts Receivable and to Accounts Payable, under the plan by which only discounts actually taken or given are entered on the books.

(*a*) Enter the transactions of Problem 85 in such a way that contra discounts shall be used.

(*b*) Enter them so that no transfers need be made from one side of the cash book to the other.

[In either case the Discounts Taken should be credited $57, and the Discounts Given should be debited $62.]

### 91

Using a purchase journal somewhat similar to that on page 376 or that on page 377, a sales journal somewhat similar to that on page 379, and a cash book somewhat similar to that on page 371 or that on page 373 (with additional columns where feasible), make the entries, post the books, and take a trial balance, for the transactions of Problem 24.

### 92

Show the deposit ledger, the discount register, the cash book, and the general ledger for these bank items:

Jan. 15. The balance of deposits at the beginning of business for the day is for Brown, $5,000; for Gray, $2,000; for White,

$6,000.[1] On that day Gray deposits $2,970, which happens to be a check drawn on this bank by Brown.

Feb. 7. A note for $3,000 signed by White, dated January 15, payable in two months, is discounted by the bank for Brown (discount $19), and is credited to Brown's account. Another note for $1,000 signed by White, dated December 15, payable in three months, is discounted for Gray (discount $6.33), and is credited to Gray's account.

March 15. White pays the two notes, which the bank holds against him, by a check on the bank itself. A note of Green for $1,000 dated February 15, payable in two months, is discounted (discount $5), and a cashier's check is given for it. The cashier's check is paid.

Show the trial balance at the close for the items given.

[The trial balance of ledger balances will have four items and a total of $13,005.00.]

## 93

A cashier found on receiving the statement of his account with his bank that the bank's balance did not agree with his check-book balance. He proceeded, of course, to reconcile the two sets of figures. The difference between the two sets of figures one month later was even greater. He found no mistake in either set of figures, and therefore was able to reconcile the two sets for both dates.

The check-book figures for the month of January were as shown below, for the balance was shown on the check book after each check was drawn and after each deposit was made. Numbers indicate checks drawn, and fractional expressions, as 1/27, indicate dates.

[1] Assume the corresponding cash to be on hand.

| | | | |
|---|---|---|---|
| Check book bal. 1/1 . . | $1,290.24 | Brought forward . . | $1,842.82 |
| #621 . . . . . . | 250.00 | Deposit 1/15 . . . . . . | 366.99 |
| | 1,040.24 | | 2,209.81 |
| #622 . . . . . . | 50.00 | #625 . . . . | 701.25 |
| | 990.24 | | 1,508.56 |
| Interest . . . . . . . . | 22.45 | Deposit 1/25 . . . . . . | 410.78 |
| | 1,012.69 | | 1,919.34 |
| Deposit 1/5 . . . . . | 597.45 | #626 . . . . | 25.00 |
| | 1,610.14 | | 1,894.34 |
| #623 . . . . . . | 1,000.00 | #627 . . . . | 416.67 |
| | 610.14 | | 1,477.67 |
| Deposit 1/7 . . . . . | 525.30 | #628 . . . . | 59.78 |
| | 1,135.44 | | 1,417.89 |
| Deposit 1/11 . . . . | 711.38 | #629 . . . . | 50.00 |
| | 1,846.82 | | 1,367.89 |
| #624 . . . . . . | 4.00 | #630 . . . . | 33.33 |
| Carried forward . | 1,842.82 | Balance 2/1 . . . . . . | 1,334.56 |

The bank statement for January was as follows:

| | | | | |
|---|---|---|---|---|
| Balance 12/30 . . . | $1,556.26 | Check | #618 . . . . | $132.06 |
| Deposit . . . . . . . . | 687.68 | | #622 . . . . | 50.00 |
| | 597.45 | | #625 . . . . | 701.25 |
| | 525.30 | | #615 . . . . | 497.66 |
| | 711.38 | | #619 . . . . | 29.95 |
| | 366.99 | | #623 . . . . | 1,000.00 |
| | 419.28 | | #621 . . . . | 250.00 |
| Interest . . . . . . . . | 2.50 | | #617 . . . . | 48.78 |
| | | | #624 . . . . | 4.00 |
| | 4,866.84 | | #616 . . . . | 209.80 |
| | | | #620 . . . . | 13.00 |
| | | Charge for collection | | .25 |
| | | No signature[1] . . . . . | | 8.50 |
| | | | | 2,945.25 |
| | | Balance 1/30 . . . . . . | | 1,921.59 |
| | | | | 4,866.84 |

Reconcile the check-book figures to the bank figures, by proper additions and subtractions (in memorandum only), for the beginning of the month; and reconcile the bank figures to the check-book figures for the end of the month.

Explain what presumably happened with respect to the no-signature check.

[Lumping in one sum all items of the same sort (though they should be shown in detail in a separate schedule), the adjustments necessary for reconciliation at the beginning of the month are three in number. The number at the end of the month is the same.]

[1] A check was deposited though lacking the signature of the customer and hence was returned and charged back.

# APPENDIX B, I

## OPENING CORPORATION BOOKS

[Pages 401–407]

### 94

A corporation is organized from two partnerships. The property of each partnership was appraised especially for the new organization, and the balance sheets resulting were as follows:

*Assets*

| | A. & B. | C. D. & Co. |
|---|---|---|
| Real Estate | $50,000 | $100,000 |
| Accounts Receivable | 15,000 | 26,000 |
| Merchandise | 46,000 | 53,000 |
| Fixtures | 4,000 | 5,000 |
| | $115,000 | $184,000 |

*Liabilities*

| | | |
|---|---|---|
| Proprietors | $90,000 | $75,000 |
| Accounts Payable | 5,000 | 15,000 |
| Bills Payable | 5,000 | 40,000 |
| Allowance for Bad Debts | 3,000 | 5,000 |
| Undivided Profit Reserve | 12,000 | 49,000 |
| | $115,000 | $184,000 |

The new corporation takes over both the assets and the liabilities of each business at par; it is agreed that the good will of C. D. & Co. is worth $25,000 and that of A. & B. is worth $20,000; and stock is issued to each on those bases. To raise cash, for none is transferred by the old partnerships, subscriptions are received for $29,000 of stock at 105, and one installment, of one half the total, is paid in cash.

Show the balance sheet of the corporation at this stage.

[Thirteen items will appear on the balance sheet, and the amount of each side will be $374,450.]

## 95

The net assets are on the books of a business at $250,000.

It is decided to form a corporation with a capitalization of $400,000. The old proprietor is to be given $275,000 in stock, and $25,000 in cash.

Stock is subscribed for by outsiders to the amount of $75,000, at par, in two installments of $37,500 each.

The first installment of subscriptions is paid.

The original proprietor transfers his business and is given his stock and cash.

New subscribers now subscribe for $50,000 of stock at 110, in two installments of $27,500 each (installments #3 and #4).

Installment #2 is paid and the stock is issued.

Installment #3 is paid.

Stock with a par value of $25,000 is donated to the corporation.

The donated stock is sold at $80 a share (par value $100).

Show the balance sheet at this point.

[The total should be $425,000 with four items on each side, counting the old assets as one item.]

## APPENDIX B, II

## CLOSING BY JOURNAL ENTRIES

[Pages 407–409]

### 96

Make the entries through the journal for closing the books of a business which yields the following figures:

*Trial Balance*

| | Dr. | Cr. |
|---|---|---|
| Cash | $175,000 | $170,000 |
| Merchandise | 138,000 | 128,000 |
| Accounts Receivable | 148,000 | 126,000 |
| Accounts Payable | 137,000 | 141,000 |
| Real Estate | 35,000 | 2,000 |
| Fixtures | 8,000 | 1,000 |
| Depreciation | 4,000 | |
| Expense | 23,000 | |
| Interest | 1,500 | 500 |
| Commission | 1,000 | 2,000 |
| Proprietor | | 100,000 |
| | $670,500 | $670,500 |

*Inventories*

| | |
|---|---|
| Merchandise | $57,000 |
| Supplies | 200 |
| Real Estate | 33,000 |
| Fixtures | 7,000 |

*Accrued*

| | |
|---|---|
| Interest resource | $200 |
| Commission liability | 100 |

*Prepaid*

| | |
|---|---|
| Insurance (charged to expense) | $100 |

[Total of new balance sheet, $124,500.]

## 97

The net inventory of merchandise at the beginning of the year was $53,000. The sales were $367,000, and the returned sales $17,000. The purchases were $215,000, and the returned purchases $3,000. The discounts given were $7,000, and the discounts taken $8,000. Enter all items given above as ledger balances on the books, each in an account by itself. The gross inventory at the end of the year was $46,000, but depreciation of $9,000 was deemed necessary. Make journal entries to carry all these items into Merchandise as a clearing account; and show the new net inventory on an inventory account for the new year.

[Test by independent figuring the correctness of your final figure for profit and loss and for the inventory account.]

# APPENDIX C

## SINGLE ENTRY

### 98

Single entry books showed the following balances at the beginning of a year: Proprietor, Cr. $55,000; Accounts Payable, Cr. $27,000; Accounts Receivable, Dr. $38,000.

The cash book showed $7,000. The inventory of goods showed $33,000, and of fixtures and supplies $4,000.

A year later, without any closing of the books in the interim, the amounts (in the same order of items as before) were as follows: $52,000, $25,000, $36,000, $9,000, $35,000, $3,000.

What was the profit or the loss for the year ?

Where was the profit, or what kind of loss had been suffered ?

[The amount of profit or of loss was $6,000.]

### 99

On a set of books all the accounts relating to the two partners are at the end of a year as follows: A's capital account, credit balance, $34,000; B's capital account, credit balance, $28,000; A's salary account, debit balance, $4,000; B's salary account, debit balance, $4,000; A's interest account, credit balance, $1,700; B's interest account, credit balance, $1,400. The partners have not yet been credited for salaries provided by the partnership agreement ($4,000 each), and as the books are kept by single entry no nominal account has been debited for the partners' interest. The assets and outside liabilities are as follows: cash, $12,000; merchandise, $25,000; fixtures, $2,000; accounts receivable, $35,000; accounts payable, $5,000.

What was the profit or the loss subsequent to the previous closing of the books ?

[The amount of profit or of loss was $3,900. Is this counting interest and salaries as costs or as profits ?]

# APPENDIX E

## PETTY CASH AND VOUCHER SYSTEMS

### 100

(1) The petty-cash account is debited for $50.00 at the time the petty-cash drawer is established. The following payments are made from petty cash: telegrams, $22.67; car fares, $13.18; laundry, $1.58; newspapers and magazines, $2.10; express, $9.15. Then the petty-cash drawer is replenished by a new amount, the intention being to keep the petty-cash "bank" approximately constant.

Make the entries for all these transactions by each of the three common methods of handling petty cash, and show the petty-cash account in the general ledger for each.

[Test the correctness of your work by considering what will actually be in the petty-cash drawer.]

(2) Enter in the voucher register all the items not merchandise for which payment was made in Problem 24, but treat the date of payment in that problem as the date of incurring the debt. Use the voucher register as a principal book. Assume payment for all items entered to be made ten days later. Enter in the cash book all payments falling within the month (on the dating plan indicated above), but leave unpaid all items going over into the next month.

[Test the accuracy of your work by the balance of Vouchers Payable.]

Bei Fragen zur Produktsicherheit wenden Sie sich bitte an:
If you have any questions regarding product safety,
please contact:

Walter de Gruyter GmbH
Genthiner Straße 13
10785 Berlin
productsafety@degruyterbrill.com